How to
Communicate
Like a
Buddhist

HOW TO
COMMUNICATE
LIKE A
BUDDHIST

CYNTHIA KANE

Hierophant publishing

Cover design by Emma Smith
Cover art © Steinar | Shutterstock
Interior design by Steve Amarillo

Hierophant Publishing
8301 Broadway, Suite 219
San Antonio, TX 78209
888-800-4240
www.hierophantpublishing.com

If you are unable to order this book from your local bookseller,
you may order directly from the publisher.

Library of Congress control number: 2016931680

ISBN: 978-1-938289-51-4

10 9 8 7 6 5 4 3 2 1

Printed on acid-free paper in the United States of America

This book is dedicated to you, the reader.
May it show up for you when you need it most.

Before you speak,
let your words pass through three gates.

At the first gate,
ask yourself, "Is it true?"

At the second gate,
ask, "Is it necessary?"

At the third gate,
ask, "Is it kind?"

—Sufi saying

Contents

Introduction

Don't try to use what you learn from Buddhism to be a Buddhist; use it to be a better whatever-you-already-are.

—Dalai Lama

For many years I relied on others as a communication style. What I mean is I rarely expressed any of my needs or wants, thinking that others would just be able to pick up on them. I would pretend everything was fine, say yes when I really wanted to say no, or go along with what I knew others wanted to hear. Never expressing myself meant I was bubbling with passive-aggressive quips, all the time frustrated and reacting because my needs weren't being met. Ask me then what the issue was, and I would've blamed everyone else. Ask me now, and I'd tell you it was that I didn't understand what real communication looked like, and how paying attention to my words, being aware of what I was saying while I was saying it, and observing without judgment could change my relationship to myself and others.

I was a product of what I was surrounded by. My teachers growing up were first and foremost my parents and other family members, but this isn't a statement of blame, as they were simply doing what they'd learned to do from their families, and their families' families, and on it goes. The other educators in my life were my friends and boyfriends, and from them I picked up habits from their communication trees. When I finally took notice of my communication style, I realized none of it was actually mine!

Think for a minute about your default style of communicating. Maybe you have habits that include selectively listening, talking over others to make a point, knowing better than others, interrupting, complaining, shutting down and walking away, or taking the role of the victim. Or maybe you've not stopped to think about how you communicate. If this describes you, don't worry— you're not alone. Many of us are walking around with a communication routine that we're unaware of. We've performed it so many times it's embedded in our day-to-day lives without us even realizing it's there or knowing it's ours. Sometimes it's possible words are coming out of our mouths and we're not really sure what we're saying, or we give a facial expression and we only become aware that we've done so because the person we're with points it out to us. But as with any aspect of our personality, we can change it if it's no longer proving useful.

This book came out of my own need to redefine my communication style. To rework how I interacted with the world around me and communicated with others and myself. When I looked closely, I saw that my default methods of communication led me to interact with others in a way that was completely out of step with what I really wanted.

Although I wanted to be open and understanding, and compassionate, and celebrate others, all I could do was react from a place of insecurity because I felt like others' goodness took away from mine, or their successes somehow made mine further out of reach. Comparing myself to others made me even more reactionary, pushing me to be passive-aggressive and blame others for what I wasn't feeling or doing. If a girl I knew looked pretty, well, that meant I looked ugly. If a friend of mine just got published in the *New York Times*, well, that meant I was further away from achieving something similar. A friend got engaged, well, that meant I was never going to find someone to love.

So what changed? One of my best friends tragically passed away, and with his passing the world looked different. What I saw was that life was too beautiful to be upset all the time, constantly comparing, competing, thinking this is right that is wrong. Life was too unpredictable to disrespect others and myself with my interactions. Life was to be enjoyed, not to suffer through. I craved to feel present, to enjoy my time here. I read books, took courses, signed up for workshops, all on this quest to care for myself; to understand how to feel good in my day-to-day. And no matter the class, or teacher, or mentor, over and over again I found that the root of my unhappiness and insecurity came from how I communicated. How I talked with others and myself dictated so much of my feeling state that to really enjoy each moment, to be here now, I had to teach myself a new way of interacting.

My search lead me to the Shambhala Meditation Center of New York, where I learned about Buddhism's four elements of right speech. When I first heard about this it was like my internal oven timer had gone off, as I knew I could use these principles as a base for communicating. Remember, you don't have to be a Buddhist to communicate like one, as the benefits of doing so are available to everyone.

The four elements are rules of communication, and over the last five years I have modernized and melded them with other forms of mindful, nonviolent, and what I call *self-responsible communication* to create a working practice. Changing how I communicated with others and myself helped me in so many ways: it increased my self-esteem, reduced stress and anxiety, and even improved my sleeping habits; it helped me understand my own feelings and the feelings of others, enhanced my appreciation for life, reduced reactivity and compulsive behavior, and helped me identify my wants and clarify goals. Changing the way I communicated helped me to create a more calm, balanced, and energized life. Through my communication practice I've become a better friend, daughter, sister, wife, aunt, employee, and coworker without sacrificing my own happiness in the process. My hope for you is that by changing the way you communicate you too can change your life and the lives of others.

What This Book Will Teach You

In the beginning, I'll explain the traditional Buddhist elements of right speech, as they are foundational. The rest of the book is devoted to my own concrete practice that I have developed over the past five years. As you will see in the following pages, creating a new communication routine begins by making small changes. Many of the examples cover small communication topics, because what I've found is that by making changes in the smaller day-to-day conversations, we are better prepared to communicate more effectively when larger life issues come up. Also, if we master our day-to-day interactions, we can potentially prevent some of the larger communication issues from even arising!

The first part will help you identify what type of communicator you are right now. This will help you see exactly what you need to work on and how this book can help transform your communication routine. I'll then introduce the elements of right speech.

Next, we'll dive into the concrete five-step practice I have developed for altering our communication routines. Because change always must start from within, I'll first ask you to begin listening more closely to yourself. Then we'll move into how to listen to others. With the tools for effective listening in place, then we get into learning to speak consciously, concisely, and clearly. We'll also apply the Buddhist principles of mindfulness and spaciousness to communication by discussing silence as a part of speech. Then we move into the last element needed to communicate like a Buddhist: meditation. Once through the five-step practice, I'll share with you the thought process of communicating in this new way and how by asking yourself a handful of questions you can turn any interaction into one that is kind, honest, and helpful.

Your life is one long conversation, so throughout the book you'll see Cultivate Communication exercises that invite you to practice some of the ideas we'll be discussing. I encourage you to pick up a journal if you don't have one already, as there will be many opportunities for you to reflect on current and past situations, and how you might communicate differently in the future. I've also found that journaling helps me to be a better communicator not just for its help with reflecting on the past, but it also helps me assign words to sometimes complex or difficult emotions. If I can articulate how I'm feeling on the page, it helps me to later express myself in conversations. At the end of each part I've included a What You Need to Remember section for easy reference.

Perhaps you picked up this book because you want to learn how to more accurately say what you mean and express how you feel; or maybe you're looking to mend old relationships, begin new ones, or you're interested in learning how to handle difficult conversations. Maybe you've realized that the way you've been interacting with others needs to change, and you want a starter guide, basic steps you can take to change your communication style now. The good news is that this book can satiate all of these desires. What you'll learn here can help you with your communication at home, work, with your friends and family, as well as in your intimate relationships. I can teach you these things because I too have struggled with learning how to speak so that I am heard and how to listen with presence and without judgment, and the teachings here describe ways in which to do exactly that.

Before we begin I want to make one thing clear: just like any sport, activity, or art form, being a good communicator takes practice. It's something we can all get better at no matter our starting point. I have never met a "perfect" communicator, and this includes me, because even after years of working with this process, I always find areas to improve upon.

I'm so thrilled that you've picked up this book and are ready to try a new way of communicating. By taking this one step you are opening yourself up to a new way of seeing yourself, others, and the world. This work isn't easy, but if I can do it I know you can too.

What's Your Communication Style?

Raise your words, not voice. It is rain that
grows flowers, not thunder.

—Rumi

To move beyond your routine patterns and begin to communicate differently, you first have to identify what kind of communicator you are. Like many spiritual traditions, Buddhism advocates meeting yourself where you are, realistically assessing your strengths and weaknesses, and plotting where you want to go. It's important to know what your communication style is right now so you can see how it evolves over the course of the coming weeks and months. The following quiz will help define your communication style and also identify how this book can help you on your journey to healthy communication.

A few words of advice to start: it's possible that you may take this quiz and discover that you are already a proficient communicator; even if this is so, try to enter with a curious mind, as there is bound to be something new to you in these pages. Don't rush through the quiz. Take your time and contemplate to what extent each question may apply to you. This is an opportunity to be open and honest with yourself about your past communications. Finally, record your answers in the margin or in your journal, as you'll be tallying your responses at the end of the quiz. Please answer each item with the following: Never, Rarely, Sometimes, Often, or Always.

1. If you feel attacked or criticized, do you criticize back?

2. Do you think you know what others are thinking?

3. Do you roll your eyes or make other physical gestures to demonstrate that you don't agree with something?

4. Do you compare yourself to others?

5. When someone shares a problem with you, do you immediately offer ways to solve it, or give advice?

6. Do you feel responsible for other people's feelings?

7. Do you say yes when you want to say no?

8. Do you take what others say personally?

9. Do you lie?

10. Do you exaggerate?

11. Do you gossip or talk badly about people behind their backs?

12. Do you talk down to people?

13. Do you pretend everything is fine when it's not?

14. Do find yourself interrupting others when they're speaking?

15. Do you make fun of others?

16. Do you use words to exert your dominance or superiority over others?

17. Do you approach conversations with a sense of right or wrong?

18. Do you expect to get what you want by controlling situations?

19. When you're listening to others, does your mind wander?

20. Do you find it difficult to express your feelings and needs?

Add up your answers: Always = 1 point; Often = 2 points; Sometimes = 3 points; Rarely = 4 points: Never = 5 points.

Always_____

Often _____

Sometimes _____

Rarely _____

Never _____

Total _____

Results

Score 78 and Up: Clear Communicator

You understand that clear communication requires empathy and understanding. You're aware of the give-and-take within a conversation and how to handle criticism without taking it personally. You believe that for there to be good communication you must be honest, use helpful language, and not gossip about others. You're aware of the value of your words, and at the same time you understand that everyone you talk to is an equal; they want the same as you: to be heard, seen, understood, and acknowledged.

Use this book to refine and perfect your communication skills. Practice applying the techniques to your day-to-day life, and in so doing nurture and support your communication style while helping others become better communicators as well.

Score 63–77: Partly Cloudy Communicator

While you're on the right path, there are still some blockages that get in your way, making it feel like you sometimes can take two steps forward and two steps back. Your drive and passion is there to learn to overcome what's holding you back, but it's time to step up the practice. The more you turn paying attention to your speech into a habit, the more you will be able to express how you feel, ask for what you want, listen to others, and respond to situations instead of react to them.

This book is going to help you with all of the above. What I've found is that those who self-test at this level benefit immensely from the first section, where you will learn how to release old stories of lack you've been telling yourself and instead see yourself with kind eyes. Many in this category also benefit from the section on listening to others, as how you interpret information can shift when you implement this practice. Finally, learning how to consciously choose your words and express yourself with clarity will take your communication skills to the next level.

Score 62 and Under: Cloudy Communicator

This was where I started: often closing off instead of sharing how I truly felt, reactive rather than responsive to the words of others, and passive-aggressive instead of assertive and clear. I would judge others and compare my insides to their outsides, which always resulted in a tirade of negative self-talk. While this was a hard place to start from, it also meant that I had the most to gain by changing my communication habits. The fact that you have picked up this book means that you too are ready to make a change. You want to learn how to communicate so that it feels good to you, so that you interact with others in a way that leaves you feeling satisfied and calm. Finally, you want to learn how to articulate yourself, knowing that you are capable of meeting your own needs.

This book is going to challenge you, maybe take you outside of your comfort zone. All I ask is that you are gentle with yourself throughout the process. This is a practice, which means you can take it slow and develop these new habits over time. I encourage you to do all the exercises and really make room for these steps in your life. It isn't easy to let yourself be uncomfortable, but I promise the discomfort will lead you to a new view of yourself and your ability to communicate.

No matter where you fall in the above breakdown, one of the basic tenets of Buddhism teaches that you're exactly where you're supposed to be. When I first got clear on my own communication style, I felt depressed and confused. I remember sitting on my couch thinking, *Geez, what do I do now?* I'd been interacting the same way for thirty-plus years, and it suddenly seemed like everything I'd been saying and doing or not saying and doing was what had been holding me back. That realization was all well and good, but where in the world was I to begin interacting with others and myself differently? How was that going to happen?

Serendipitously, I received what I thought at the time was a rather random e-mail from a friend about a writing and meditation workshop at the Shambhala Meditation Center of New York. For some reason I was moved to sign up, and it was there that I discovered the four elements of right speech. When I heard them listed and explained I knew I'd found a guide for communication that I could use. It became a way to easily see what I needed to get rid of, to keep, or to add to my communication routine.

Every interaction we have can be seen through the lens of these four elements. In the next section I'll explain what they are and go through each of them in detail.

The Four Elements of Right Speech

In March 2011, I sat on the floor of my apartment in New York City, fumbling for my tissues. My best friend had passed away unexpectedly. He was kayaking and got caught in a swell on a river in Costa Rica. For months all I could do was lay or sit on my floor, cry, and blow out the pain into tissues or (most of the time) toilet paper. There I was, on my floor, when I read about what in Mahayana Buddhism is known as a *bodhisattva*: essentially an enlightened person who's dedicated to alleviating others' suffering.

I put the book to the side, lay on my back, and looked up to the ceiling. Where was *my* bodhisattva? Where was the person who could help alleviate my suffering? I thought on this for a while, as most of my life I'd hoped for someone to come along and make me feel better or somehow make me feel worthy and deserving, good. And even though I'd put the responsibility in others' laps all my life and had never found anything but disappointment, here I was doing it yet again. I sat up.

Maybe I didn't need to find an enlightened being, but rather learn what made someone enlightened. If I could understand the way of the bodhisattva, maybe I could incorporate some of their qualities into my own life to take away my suffering. So I read. And I read some more. And soon I formed an image in my mind, a kind of mental map of what a bodhisattva embodied. I jotted down words, actions—all the things I associated with a bodhisattva.

There are many definitions of a bodhisattva that are more detailed than mine, but what I concluded was that a bodhisattva sees clearly, speaks honestly, understands pain and suffering, practices compassion, sees everyone as equals, and, most importantly, wants to help others. It is a way of being that aims to eliminate suffering, and I saw how mindfulness and right speech are primary practices used to help reach this goal.

🌸 Mindfulness

Mindfulness means paying attention to what we're doing while we're doing it—without judgment. In Buddhism, there is what's known as mindful speech. Mindful speech is the practice of bringing our attention to our words. It means we are aware of what we're saying while we're saying it. It is a practice of observation and not evaluation. It is paying attention on purpose, with a moment-to-moment awareness. We'll start applying mindfulness practices when we get into the five steps to change how we communicate.

While various teachers and schools of Buddhism translate the four elements of right speech in slightly different ways, there is one thing they all agree on: right speech is a guideline for communicating in a loving, compassionate, and authentic way. I teach the elements of right speech as the following:

- Tell the truth.
- Don't exaggerate.
- Don't gossip.
- Use helpful language.

I'll explain all of these in greater detail in a moment.

Another tool we will utilize are three questions, and they act like a litmus test as to whether or not our words are following the principle of right speech. When in doubt about any statement, if you can answer yes to all of the following questions then it's likely your words are consistent with the principles of right speech:

- Is what I am about to say true?
- Is what I am about to say kind?
- Is what I am about to say helpful?

We'll come back to these four principles and the above three questions again and again, as they act as filters from which all our speaking and listening pour through. If we can incorporate these principles into our day-to-day interactions, we not only learn how to speak and listen in a way that helps others and ourselves suffer less, but we also have a checklist to make sure we're clearly communicating.

Tell the Truth

If I asked you if you are reading a book right now, you would say yes. If I asked you what color your shirt is, you'd likely tell me exactly what I see. These are easy truths to express. But what about the harder truths, like when a friend asks if you like her partner and you say yes when you really want to say no? Or your boss asks if you want to take on another project and you really don't but you do it anyway? How do we state those truths?

Let's face it. A lot of the time we don't tell the truth. In a word, we lie. Sometimes we lie because we don't want to offend anybody, or come off as needy, mean, demanding, or even confrontational. Other times we lie because we are afraid of what people will think of us if we tell the truth, or that if we tell the truth then we won't get something we want, or we will lose something we already have, whether that be a material possession or an image we have created and are trying to maintain. If we look at the majority of our lies, the root behind them is desire and fear.

Perhaps we tell ourselves that the issue we're lying about isn't that important. Plus, it can be scary to reveal how we truly feel without knowing what others' reactions may be. On the other hand, maybe we've tried to be honest many times but nobody's getting it, and so we choose to tell people what they want to hear instead of the truth. But by burying the truth of how we feel, what we're really doing is being dishonest with ourselves. If we hide the truth one time, and then another, and so on, it compounds over time to create a life of dissatisfaction and resentment.

I understand that sometimes telling the truth is hard—especially when our goal is to protect someone's feelings. That begs the question, is there a way we can be truthful and also mindful of how our words will likely be interpreted? Are white lies acceptable when our aim is to serve the greater good? Questions like these are difficult to answer, and my experience is that very few people are able to give up speaking untruths altogether. But if we can become mindful of when, where, and most importantly why we lie, we have taken the first step toward eliminating or at least minimizing them from our communications.

Personally, I have a habit of lying to others about my own wants and needs, especially when it comes to intimate relationships. I like to pretend everything is hunky dory when it really isn't. Why? Because I want to avoid conflict; I want to be able to go with the flow. But here's what happens when I do that: I don't honor my own truth. I keep myself in the same position of lack. I suffer, and in turn so does my partner. Let's look at a quick example.

I pretend it's fine that my partner is going out with his friends instead of coming to family dinner. (I'm lying.)

My partner thinks I'm telling the truth, so he goes out with his friends.

I'm angry that he went out with his friends, so when he gets home I'm passive-aggressive, saying that I'm fine. Really. Nothing's wrong. (Again, I'm lying.)

Both people suffer. I suffer because I'm not getting what I want. He suffers because I'm now being mean to him.

We will talk more about this graphic in a later section on the language of silence and passive-aggressive behavior. But for now, just notice it as a little example of not being truthful.

When we say what we mean, we signal to ourselves that we believe our truth; that we are capable of taking care of our own needs; that we are ultimately responsible for turning our desires into action. By being clear about our needs, we accept the reality of how we feel and can choose to alleviate our own suffering. If we choose to ignore or hide the truth, this almost inevitably leads to us acting in ways that promote hurtful interactions. The times when it's difficult to be honest are generally the moments when honesty is needed most—to help clear tension, to release our feelings, to gain acceptance of ourselves and others, and to liberate us from resentment and shame.

Depending on the situation, being honest can be uncomfortable, so we get comfortable with it by learning how to tell the truth in an effective way. If we aren't careful, saying what we mean can come across as hurtful, attacking, criticizing, or judging. This is not effective communication. But if we focus on our own needs and not the actions that provoke them, we make it easier for the person we're speaking with to hear us. If we come from a place of observation without judgment it's likely the person we're with will feel safe enough to respond instead of getting defensive, shutting down, or even running for the hills. We will look at effective ways to do this throughout the book.

Don't Exaggerate

The next three rules come out of the first rule.

Before I learned the second rule, don't exaggerate, many things in my life were a big deal. I'd take one critical remark and interpret it to mean that I was the worst person in the world. Or, in the other direction, I would take a positive remark and think I was better or knew more than those I was working with. When I'd want to sound important, I'd talk about how much I had going on and how there was no way I could go out for dinner because I was way too busy. And when I was in catastrophe mode, I would typically collapse on my couch with boxes of Chinese food, wallowing in negative self-talk and thinking the worst-case scenarios in all areas of my life.

The second element of right speech is related to the first, as anytime we are exaggerating, we aren't telling the truth or seeing the situation for what it is—we're lying to others and ourselves. When we fall into a habit of exaggerating, we often alternate between either being horrible people or perfect saints; we never see others and ourselves as equals.

This second rule of right speech can be related to another Buddhist principle: equanimity. Equanimity, or the art of staying balanced, is one of four principal virtues that the Buddha encouraged his disciples to cultivate. These virtues are referred to as the four immeasurables. The others are metta (loving-kindness), compassion, and sympathetic joy. Any time we exaggerate, we are by definition out of balance.

When it comes to exaggeration, many people can spot the obvious examples, such as when someone exaggerates to seem more "important" (Buddhism is clear that no one is more important than anyone else), or wealthier than he or she actually is. But it's the more subtle examples of exaggeration that many of us miss, likely because we don't see them as exaggerations. Take a look at the following statements:

- "This is the worst day of my life."
- "You always do that to me."
- "This is taking forever."
- "I will never get out of here."
- "I can't believe you would do/say that."
- "This place has the worst service on the planet."
- "He/she is always late."
- "That was a complete waste of my time."
- "Someone like him/her would never be interested in someone like me."

In most cases, all of these statements are likely exaggerations, and consequently not helpful in terms of developing good communication habits with others and yourself. Take a look at the last one, "Someone like him/her would never be interested in someone like me." When you say something like this, not only have you exaggerated, but you have also put forth the implication (to yourself) that you are "not good enough" for the other person. Statements of exaggeration, especially negative ones, carry the energy of suffering with them that can discolor your experience of the moment. (We will cover this in more detail in the section "Listen to Yourself.")

By coming to a conversation with a sense of equanimity and equality instead of exaggeration, you can avoid many of the pitfalls of miscommunication. Instead of making blanket statements that demean your worthiness or provoke a defensive or antagonistic reaction in someone (and also aren't true in most cases), you are more likely to create an environment where positive feelings and genuine communication can take place.

Even when you are in a communication scenario with someone who isn't likely to bring a sense of equanimity and equality, if you can be the one to be mindful of your words and actions, then you have the tools to help create a positive communication experience. Here are some ways you can prevent exaggerating in your conversations:

- Pay attention to words that overemphasize the negative of a situation or the positive of a situation.
- Pay attention to your reactions. Are they over the top? Is everything the worst possible scenario? Is everything the best possible scenario? Are you turning yourself into the victim? The victor? Is it all happening to you? Me. Me. Me. Me.

- Tap in to see if you're feeling "better than" whomever you are with, or "less than" whomever you are with, remembering that in reality this isn't possible.

Buddhism teaches that we all want the same outcome in life—to be understood, to feel good, to be happy. I have found this closely describes what we all want out of communication—to be understood, to feel good about it, and for it to lead to happiness.

We all know what it feels like to hurt and to feel joy; to feel attacked and to feel supported; to feel invisible and to feel seen; to feel frustrated and to feel fulfilled. When we can identify the feelings of others in ourselves, our conversations are more likely to become a dialogue in which the desire is to help. Being a good communicator involves describing situations and your feelings about those situations as accurately as possible, and not exaggerating is a crucial component of this. Developing a practice that replaces exaggeration with equanimity is a good first step on the path.

Don't Gossip

The third rule of right speech, don't gossip, actually runs contrary to what most of us see in our everyday lives. From celebrity websites, television shows, and magazines that beckon our attention in the grocery store checkout line, spreading information about others has become a regular part of daily life for many, not to mention a multimillion-dollar industry. With so much of it going on around us all the time, it's easy to dismiss gossiping about others as acceptable.

And while celebrity gossip is easy to identify, gossip in our personal lives comes in many different forms, including things such as repeating something someone told you in confidence, sharing an assumption of others' lives, or telling others about an issue you have with someone instead of addressing the problem directly. Ranging from small comments about a coworker's performance, to complaining to your friends about your significant other or sharing stories that you were asked to keep private, for many people gossiping is so prevalent that they no longer notice it as such.

Some of us see gossiping as a method of bonding with others, and because of this we perpetuate the idea that gossiping is beneficial. Gossiping can quickly become habit-forming as the rush of being the one "in the know" can make us feel important, and we might find it hard to keep future information to ourselves. This need to express everything the minute it comes in means there's little consideration given to whether what we have to say is kind, true, and helpful. Take the following example:

Jennifer calls and tells you that she and her husband are having problems. She says they are going to start therapy.

You get off the phone and call Susan to tell her what Jennifer just told you.

Susan calls Kerry and tells her that Jennifer and her husband are having problems. They speculate—maybe he's having an affair; neither of them have seen them together in a while.

At the block party Jennifer and her husband show up together. Susan and Kerry stand over by the side and whisper and stare. Neither could imagine staying with their husbands if they cheated. What is she thinking?

Much like exaggeration, gossip creates a sense that you are either "better than" or "worse than" those you gossip about (typically the former). I believe that most gossip stems from envy, as at some point in the past we have been envious of the person we are now gossiping about. This is fairly obvious when it comes to celebrity gossip, as when famous people are shown to have normal human issues and shortcomings, we rejoice in the fact that they aren't so "special" after all.

When we see our gossiping as a product of envy, we can instead challenge ourselves to replace it with one or two of the other four immeasurables mentioned earlier in this chapter, sympathetic joy and compassion.

Sympathetic joy is the practice of celebrating the accomplishments, achievements, or good tidings that come to another. This practice can be easy to do when it's your children or other close family members you are rejoicing on behalf of. But it can be more difficult to rejoice for those who receive a benefit that you wanted for yourself. For instance, if a coworker gets a project or promotion you were hoping to receive, notice if you have a desire to gossip or belittle their achievement. If you do, instead make a conscious choice to celebrate his or her success instead. As you can imagine, this isn't easy to do, but I can tell you that the benefits of practicing sympathetic joy instead of gossip are profound. Try it for yourself and see what happens!

On the other side of the coin, instead of gossiping when others experience suffering, Buddhism invites us to bring compassion to the situation instead. In terms of communication, this can be applied by replacing words that make fun of or rejoice in the hard times that have befallen another with words that express compassion for those affected. Depending on the situation and our feelings about it, it may be that the best we can do to practice compassion is to remain silent when the opportunity to gossip presents itself—but even this is a big improvement on participating in gossiping, and it moves us more in alignment with our desire to communicate like a bodhisattva.

Lastly, there are also times we gossip and internally justify it because we think we are being helpful. For instance, we may converse about one family member to another under the auspices that we are "concerned," but our real motive is not so benign. If what we're saying is grounded in judgment and personal gain rather than the intention to be truly helpful, this practice of "don't gossip" asks us to refrain from speaking at all.

But talking about others without their knowledge is sometimes inevitable, you might be thinking. If your sister wants to know how your great aunt Midge was when you visited last weekend, you will probably want to share how it went. If your boss asks how a new coworker is doing on your team, she's going to expect some kind of feedback from you. So what's the difference between gossip and simply sharing information? The easiest way to know for sure is to ask yourself, *What if the person I'm talking about heard me?* How would he or she feel? Furthermore, what energy are you creating inside yourself and others when you talk about people? The key is to never say something that you wouldn't stand behind if the person were within earshot.

If we want to get out of the gossip cycle, it takes a very disciplined approach to do so—especially if we have formed a habit to bond with friends, coworkers, and family members in this way. Below are specific questions to start asking that can help stop the wheel.

Before you share information from someone else, ask yourself:

- Is this your information to share?
- If I share this information, whom am I helping?
- Why do I want to share this information?
- If whomever this information belongs to knew I was sharing it, how would they feel?
- If a child overheard my conversation, what would he or she learn?
- Is what I am about to say disrespecting someone else?

Although not participating in gossip can be difficult if we are only beginning to realize the full extent of how we gossip in everyday communication, the good news is that in most cases it only takes one person to change the conversation. We can do this by either not engaging when gossip is presented, changing the subject, or, in some cases, specifically stating, "Let's talk about something else." In so doing, we will be on our way to practicing the third rule of right speech. When our conversations are seen through the lens of "Is what I am about to say true, kind, and helpful?" we soon realize there's no point to gossip except to maintain some illusory sense of superiority.

Use Helpful Language

The final rule of right speech, use helpful language, can perhaps best be explained and practiced by identifying and avoiding its opposite: unhelpful language.

Unhelpful language is anything that blocks or prevents either person in a conversation from understanding the other's point of view. For example, if we look at past conversations that could be described as critical, confrontational, or even heated, we're likely to see where the words used in those instances have been unhelpful.

When we begin an interaction by using words that criticize others for making mistakes, or blame them for how we feel, we have started the conversation on shaky footing. The situation is not likely to get better for us until we learn how to adjust our language. Similarly, if we raise our voice or bring a threatening tone to our words, it's difficult to imagine the rest of the conversation being productive.

Unfortunately, we can't always predict if a conversation is going to get heated or not, as sometimes we have very little time to understand what we're feeling and needing and what the other person is feeling and needing. So instead we respond defensively or aggressively, or we go the other way and sulk, get quiet, or become uncooperative.

Helpful language is when we choose words that express ourselves in such a way that others don't feel attacked or criticized. Little is gained if our words cause someone else to become defensive, or to feel as if they have to prove themselves or hide themselves. Let's look at this example:

Your friend is late is meet you at the restaurant. You're annoyed. The minute she walks up, you say, "You're always late. What's wrong with you?"

Depending on your friend, her reaction could look like: jabbing back and getting righteous; defending herself or denying her action; or shutting down, too overwhelmed.

Or

Your friend is late. When she arrives, you say, "When you're late, I feel hurt."

Because you've consciously thought about how to express yourself, your friend doesn't feel attacked, or accused of anything.

It's important to mention here that using helpful language not only applies in situations when we talk to others, but also when we talk to ourselves. It's my experience that how we talk to ourselves sets the foundation for how we speak to others. If we're always on our case for not meeting our own expectations, or judging ourselves for things that we perceive to be wrong or a mistake, it's very likely that we're going to think everyone else is judging and talking about us that way as well. The words we speak to ourselves over and over again become our beliefs, and if we are feeding ourselves a diet of negative self-talk, we create an environment of suffering.

Below is a list of descriptive phrases that people say about themselves, all of which aren't very helpful. Things like:

- "That was so dumb—I can't believe I did that."
- "Leave it to me to screw everything up!"
- "I'm sorry, this isn't going to be very good."
- "That's so like me to say I'll do something and then not follow through."
- "I'm never going to be able to afford that."

While some of these statements may not seem like obviously hurtful speech, if we look closer, we can see that, really, what we're saying to ourselves in some cases is pretty mean. In all of these instances we're telling ourselves, sometimes subtly and sometimes not, that we aren't good enough. And each time we put ourselves down, we build on the belief that we aren't worthy or deserving. There's a phrase in politics that says, "Where you stand depends on where you sit." If we sit in our insecurity and self-judgment, we stand for it as well.

Another way to think about helpful language is to consider the previously unmentioned of the four immeasurables—metta, or loving-kindness. While the first part of metta, love, gets most of the attention in our society, I would like to focus on the second part, kindness.

For instance, when someone is short, abrasive, or rude to you, how do you normally respond? For many people, the first inclination is to respond in kind instead of with kindness, but this can rarely be described as helpful.

Making a conscious decision to be kind in our responses rather than reactionary is helpful. Oftentimes this can be as simple as overlooking another person's remark and not letting it draw in our ego, instead responding in such a way that shows our intention is to be kind.

This sense of kindness can be extended to ourselves, especially when we "make a mistake" and our current habit is to unload a barrage of negative self-talk. We can start using more helpful language by paying attention to our words and the stories we're telling ourselves over and over again. This will be discussed in great detail in the next section, Listen to Yourself. If we start speaking to ourselves in a kind, honest, nonjudgmental, and helpful way, then we are far more likely to create interactions with others that follow these same rules.

. . . .

🌸 Cultivate Communication

In your journal, write the four elements of right speech with room under each one:

- Tell the truth.
- Don't exaggerate.
- Don't gossip.
- Use helpful language.

Now think a bit about the last time you didn't tell the truth, exaggerated, gossiped, and didn't use helpful language. This isn't to call you out and point fingers, but rather to get you to notice your actions, which will help you to become aware of your communication patterns. The first step to changing a behavior is to become aware of when, how, and why we do it. Start to see these moments as opportunities for change.

What to Remember

With the rules of right speech, we now have a foundational understanding of how a Buddhist communicates. She uses words that are true, balanced, necessary, and kind. She listens intently to others and to herself. And while she realizes that she is only responsible for what she says (not what others hear), she still takes great care to choose her words skillfully, so that the recipient is more likely to hear and understand them. She doesn't speak negatively about people. She speaks from the heart. And once the words are said, she lets them go.

The rules of right speech are by design simple and easy to remember. But that doesn't mean they're simple and easy to apply. At this point you may be wondering, how does this actually work? It's all good in theory, sure, but how do I apply these rules to my life? In heated discussions? How can I make sure I'm being honest, not making everything a big deal, giving up my own agenda, and choosing helpful language? The following visual shows the five steps, which we'll learn more about in the coming pages!

To Tell the Truth
To Not Exaggerate
To Not Gossip
To Use Helpful Language

Step 1: Listen to yourself

Step 2: Listen to others

Step 3: Speak consciously, concisely, and clearly

Step 4: Use the language of silence

Step 5: Meditate

Mindful Listening

Mindfulness means paying attention moment-to-moment to what we're doing while we're doing it, without judgment. In this context, mindful listening means paying attention to what we're hearing from others and ourselves. The five-step practice starts here because to change our communication routine the first thing we need to do is listen to our existing speaking patterns and identify what needs reshaping. After we change out of our old speaking garb we're then primed to listen to others in a kind, honest, and helpful way.

Listen to Yourself

If you don't communicate well with yourself,
you cannot communicate well with another person.

—Thich Nhat Hanh

Applying the rules of right speech can be very difficult if we don't start to listen to the words we use to speak to others and ourselves. If our intention is to be honest, refrain from exaggeration and gossip, and use helpful language, then we start by noticing our words and the emotions behind them. Although communication is not a one-man show, it does start with you. While you can't control what comes out of anybody else's mouth, you can become aware of what's coming out of yours, and how the words you choose affect others and yourself. By the end of the chapter you'll see that communication with others grows out of how we speak to ourselves, and through speaking to ourselves kindly and without judgment, we nurture a self that is able to speak with others in the same way.

Self-Talk

Before I learned how to communicate effectively, not only did I not notice the words I was using when I spoke to others, but I also didn't observe how mean and judgmental I was being to myself. My mother used to tell me I was my own worst critic, and it was years before I realized how right she was. For instance, if someone paid me a compliment, my first reaction was to downplay it, and often make an excuse for why I had done well. Noticing habits like this proved important, because I realized that how I speak to myself directly influences how I interact and communicate with others. Because I put myself down again and again, my self-esteem and self-confidence suffered. As a result, many of my conversations consisted of me covering up my insecurities by pretending I knew more than I did, criticizing and gossiping about others when I felt threatened by them, and then creating a story of my victimhood that I would share with my friends and, more importantly, myself.

Mindful communication starts with learning how to speak to you first. Why? Because from where you sit you stand, and from where you stand you speak. If you can't be kind, honest, and helpful in your own self-talk, it's very difficult to genuinely interact with others in the same way.

To develop a more effective communication practice, we'll be undertaking three steps:

1. Pay attention to your words and speech.

2. Pay attention to your feelings.

3. See yourself with friendly eyes.

By listening to how you speak to yourself, you'll discover your current self-communication habits. You'll identify certain words that prevent you from seeing yourself clearly and learn how to revise them. Next, you'll learn how to move away from any old stories you're telling yourself that you aren't good, smart, capable, funny, etc. by paying attention to the feelings these stories provoke. Finally, you'll practice seeing yourself with friendly attention, so that you aren't a critic but a reporter on the scene—an observer. Putting it all together can help you speak to yourself in a way that is true, kind, and helpful.

How to Listen to Yourself

 Pay attention to your words and speech.

 Pay attention to your feelings.

 See yourself with friendly eyes.

Pay Attention to Your Words and Speech

Before I learned to mindfully observe my internal and external words, I went about my day thinking more about what I had to get done, what I wanted to achieve, or what I wanted to acquire. When I wasn't in acquisition mode, I'd distract myself with television or surfing the Internet, often comparing myself to others based on their external looks or what they had accomplished. What I didn't realize was that ignoring my words was nurturing hurtful and harmful communication patterns.

Here are some communication habit examples that I discovered about myself once I began to consciously watch how I spoke to others and myself. Perhaps you will recognize a few in yourself. The point of these examples is to show you how the little ways we speak to ourselves can lay the groundwork for the larger stories that form later on.

The Complainer

My husband Bryan and I were going to New York for the weekend, and in my mind I had this idea of where we would stay, how it would look, and what it would feel like. When we arrived, I loved everything about the room: the tile floors in the bathroom, that we were on the twelfth floor and had a beautiful view of the streets below, the clean white sheets and the small breakfast table with two wire-rim chairs to relax in. And though I was giddy with delight at the smell of the shampoo and conditioner, a part of me, an old pattern part, kicked in. *It's wonderful, but there could be a bit more counter space in the bathroom. I really love it, but the pillows—well, they could have more substantial pillows.*

I call this the "but pattern": *Everything is wonderful, but . . . The food was great, but . . . We had such a great time, but . . .* I noticed how I used this little word to sabotage an otherwise good experience. I noticed how using the word "but" changed my feelings about the trip, and if I said my "but" aloud, it would affect Bryan too. But what was the truth of the situation? Was I making a bigger deal out of things than needed? Was I exaggerating the problems?

🌸 Cultivate Communication

During the day, notice if you fall into the "but pattern." If you find you do, first consider if you need to be saying "but" at all. Second, think about replacing "but" with "and." One of my clients took an improv class, and the first thing he learned to keep a scene going was the phrase, "Yes, and . . ." So one person might say, "I'm catching the next flight to Florida." And instead of a scene partner saying, "No, we're actually going to Argentina," he or she would say, "Yes, and when we get there Aunt Jane is picking us up." This phrase is additive instead of subtractive. It gives you an opportunity to create more. Although my client learned this technique in improv class, I have found that it's also a wonderful tool for communication. Try replacing "but" with "and." Instead of saying, "The food was good, but the restaurant was so loud," you'd say something like, "The food was good and the restaurant was loud."

The Apologizer

There was a time when "I'm sorry" was my most common phrase. I'd run into someone in the grocery store and say, "Sorry." A friend would ask for a Band-Aid, and I'd say, "I'm sorry, I don't have one." Someone would call, and I'd be indisposed and say, "I'm sorry, but I can't talk right now." At all points of the day, it seemed like I was apologizing for something. At home, I sat on my couch and thought about how when I had lived in Madrid, there was a big difference between *lo siento*, *permiso* or *perdón*, and *disculpe*. In Spanish, *lo siento* means "I'm sorry," and it is only used if you've actually done something hurtful. If you needed to pass by someone, you'd say *permiso* or *perdón*, which pretty much translates to "Excuse me." And if you needed to tap someone on the shoulder for something, you'd likely say, "*Disculpe*." As I sat longer and thought harder about when I would say "I'm sorry," I realized it was more of a reflex than an actual feeling of sorrow or regret. I was using "I'm sorry" in place of phrases like "excuse me" or "pardon me." By using it incorrectly and often, I was feeling bad for no good reason.

- -

🌸 Cultivate Communication

Do you apologize too much? Think about the phrase, "I'm sorry," and call to mind any past events that you are truly sorry for: I'm sorry for yelling at my daughter when I lost my patience; I'm sorry for saying something mean and reactionary to my spouse. Recognize the heaviness and implication of hurtfulness that comes with this phrase. Next, think about the phrase "excuse me" and instances when you would use it instead: in the grocery store, or moving through an aisle at a show or movie. Note how this phrase is not weighted in judgment or remorse but rather has a friendly tone of equality. How many times do you say "I'm sorry" in instances when an "excuse me" would work?

Start noticing how and when you say I'm sorry during the day. In these instances, ask yourself if an apology was necessary or if "excuse me" would have been more apt. What I've learned is that sometimes when I'm about to say I'm sorry, excuse me works better, and it's also possible that nothing needs to be said at all.

The Should

Before I began working on my internal communication, there was always a "should" in my life. I *should* be studying more. I *should* be eating right. I *should* be married with kids. I *should* be more established in my career. And on it goes. The problem with the word "should" is that it passes judgment. It implies that what we're doing at this moment isn't good enough. And who decided that I should be doing all of these things, anyway?

When I looked deeper, I realized that I was often trying to live up to other people's expectations, disguising them as my own. As a result, I was giving others the power. I learned to substitute "could" where I would normally say "should," and by doing so my internal communication began to change: I *could* be doing my PhD, and right now I'm taking a break instead. I *could* be more established in my career, and I'm choosing to take my time and make sure to enjoy my work. Furthermore, by replacing "should" with "could," we can start to see the reasons why we're not doing certain things: I could be traveling the world, and I'm choosing to stay put for a year to save money instead. I could be living closer to family, and I'm choosing to follow my dream and live in Europe instead. I could be making money working for someone else, and instead I'm choosing to start my own company.

What the above implies is that we have a choice with what we're doing and where we're putting our attention. Instead of passing judgment, and seeing ourselves locked in someone else's definition of living, we see with more clarity where we're putting our energy, and in turn we accept that the reason we're not doing X is because we're (happily) doing Y. We start to see through our own lens instead of others'.

That's Just Not Who I Am or I'm Not Good at That

I used to say "That's just not who I am" or "I'm not good at that" *a lot*. I would say it when I didn't believe in myself, when I felt stupid, or when I wanted to change and be more open and transparent but was scared to try. "I'm not good at math," I would say. "It's just not who I am." What I learned, though, was that I *could* do math. But by saying "I'm not good at that," or "That's just not who I am," I was limiting my capability to be more if I wanted to.

Noticing this phrase, I use the same exercise as I do when I'm tempted to say "should" instead of "could": I *could* be good at math, and I choose to spend my time writing instead. I *could* apply for the management position at work, and I choose to stay in my current position and enjoy more free time instead. I *could* be starting a family, and I can see that the time isn't right for that just yet.

The more we take responsibility for what we choose, as opposed to chalking it up to "how it is" or "how it's always been," the more we free ourselves from a false perception of who we are. If I had chosen to study math instead of English, I could have been a mathematician instead of an author—imagine that! What choices are you making that preclude you from doing other things? Embrace your choices instead of subtly beating yourself up for them.

. . . .

✵ Cultivate Communication

Draw a line down the middle of a page in your journal. On the left side, write down any "should" stories you have in your life, as well as any areas you have told yourself you're just not good at. On the right side, go through each item and change the should to "I could do X, and I'm choosing to . . ." By changing from should to could, notice how you are no longer using your words to beat yourself up, which means that you're seeing the truth of the situation.

I Am

When people ask us how we are, we likely respond with "I am": "I'm busy." "I'm tired." "I'm hungry." If we're asked how we're feeling, we say things like, "I'm upset." "I'm happy." What these responses all have in common is *I am*. This implies a fixed, somewhat permanent state. When we say "I am angry" or "I am sad," it suggests that we feel we are that emotion, when really the emotion is happening to us, flowing through us for a time. The verb "to be" implies an absolute that we don't always necessarily need.

The language we use is so powerful. For example, in Spanish, when someone is feeling scared, they say, *Tengo miedo*, which literally translates to "I have fear." Or someone might say *Tengo hambre*—"I have hunger." These are temporary states, fleeting, and the language used communicates this, albeit subtly. By seeing our emotions as separate from who we are, we're less likely to get stuck in the emotion and instead see it as something we can work through.

. . . .

🌸 Cultivate Communication

Pay attention to how you're using "I am" in your day to day. When you notice yourself saying "I'm frustrated/mad/upset/happy/excited/scared," try to shift your thinking. See if instead you can say, "I have anger right now"; "I have frustration"; "I have sadness." Simply restating what you feel so that it is detached from who you are can help you to see the emotion as something to work through instead of something to marinate in.

Always or Never

Much like "That's just not who I am" or "I'm not good at that," some of us have developed a habit of starting sentences with the words "I always" or "I never." But when these descriptors are used with a negative context, notice how you are offhandedly criticizing yourself in the process. Both words are definitive. They imply that there is no way to change, and there are no options to choose from. By using "always" and "never," we are telling ourselves that change is impossible.

When we use blanket statements like this, we see that we're not only being dishonest with ourselves, we're often exaggerating the situation too. Instead, what we want to do is rephrase what we're saying to make it more in line with being kind, honest, balanced, and helpful. We do this by rephrasing our language so that instead of making blanket statements about previous events, we focus on the truth of the present moment, with friendliness toward our actions and ourselves. This is right speech toward ourselves in action. Let's look at a few examples.

- "I never get to work on time," versus "I can get to work on time, and today I was late and that's okay. I can do better tomorrow."
- "I always miss deadlines," versus "I can meet deadlines, and today I missed one and that's okay. I can do better next time."
- "I never know what to do," versus "I know what to do in most cases, and right now I'm unsure and that's okay. I will give it more thought, talk to someone about it, and then make a decision."

By rephrasing these kinds of sentences we acknowledge the truth of the situation but discard any negative judgments about ourselves that were implied in the original. In the revision we note the problem, but we don't let it define us. We acknowledge it, forgive ourselves for the mistake, and know this one instance doesn't mean we're doomed to repeat the same issue again and again.

. . . .

🏵️ Cultivate Communication

Are there times that you use "always" or "never"? Who were you with? What was the context? What were the sentences? Write them down. How do they make you feel? Stuck? Pigeonholed? How can you revise the phrase so you don't feel like you're living a life sentence?

These examples of common communication patterns illustrate how the way we speak to ourselves can create or reinforce self-limiting beliefs and perceptions. In the next section, we will look at how negative self-talk can lead to entire negative narratives we tell ourselves, often without realizing how damaging this can be, and how replacing this type of negative self-talk with words grounded in right speech can transform our communication and our lives.

Know Your Stories

> *We are what we think.*
> *All that we are arises with our thoughts.*
> *With our thoughts we make the world.*
> *Speak or act with an impure mind*
> *And trouble will follow you*
> *As the wheel follows the ox that draws the cart.*

> —The Buddha, translation by Thomas Byrom

Many psychologists identify the stories we tell ourselves as the basis for our limiting beliefs. Beliefs that hold us back from experiencing love, joy, and laughter—basically, all the good stuff. The more we tell ourselves that we can't finish a project, that we're going to be single with forty cats for the rest of our lives, that good things never happen to us, or that we're always late, the more we believe the story to be true. And the more we believe it, the more we act and communicate accordingly. The more we practice this kind of negative self-talk, the more permanent our beliefs become. What I have found through teaching people how to be aware of their communication is that most of them are repeating this negative self-talk to themselves throughout the day, often without realizing the impact it has on the way they view themselves and others.

By being mindful of the way you speak to yourself about yourself, you may also notice that some of these negative thoughts and narratives may not actually be yours. In other words, a lot of what we have going on repeat in our minds is someone else's story or thought. Going back to when we were younger, we were told by our parents and those around us who we were and what was important; and as a result, a lot of what we thought about ourselves and the world was planted in us by others. I see it all the time with parents and their children: "She's tired all the time." "He doesn't like the outdoors." "She's anxious." "He doesn't like the heat." "She doesn't like to dance." And on, and on, and on. During our formative years, the stories we hear about ourselves can easily be mistaken as fact instead of opinion, and in many cases we absorb these stories as our own.

Stories are always firing in our heads, and when they are negative, they are what prevent us from taking risks; they are what keep us stuck in the same place, saying the same things again and again but hoping for a different result. Based on the examples in the previous section, it's not too hard to imagine an internal narrative like this:

Growing up, I never felt like I quite fit in. I did well in school, getting mostly As and Bs, but I was never good at math, where I got mostly Cs and an occasional B. This wasn't acceptable at all, because both my parents are mathematicians. As a result, I felt like

I constantly had to apologize when asked by them, their colleagues, and my teachers as to why my grades in math weren't better. "It's just not me," I would say, "I'm not good at math." As I got older, I avoided any jobs that required computation or accounting of any kind, because I just knew I couldn't do it right.

If you told yourself a story like this one over and over, do you think you might feel a little depressed? When you begin to notice how little communication habits of complaining, incessantly apologizing, wishing your life was different, and the countless other ways you can feed yourself a diet of negative self-talk, you can see how these habits can affect your self-perception and, in turn, your perception of others. By definition, a story filled with negative self-talk is not true, kind, or helpful to others or yourself.

Let's imagine what a story might sound like through the lens of right speech.

I was lucky to be born into a family of accomplished mathematicians. Growing up, I preferred English to math, so while I could have worked hard to become a mathematician myself, I found my true passion was for literature and writing. As a result, I was able to share with my family a perspective on these subjects that they might not have received otherwise. At first I thought they wanted me to study math too, but when we discussed it openly I learned that they want me to do whatever makes me happy. I love my parents, and it's great having people in the family who are so good at math—especially when I have a dollars-and-sense or tax-related question!

While this example is fairly simple, it describes a process of looking at events through the lens of right speech instead of unhealthy communication habits and negative self-talk that was present in the first story. This same process can be applied regardless of the nature of our personal story. We have all experienced challenges in life, difficulties, and even tragedies, but what I have found is that it's often the conversations we have with ourselves about these events that make a more lasting impact than the events themselves.

. . . .

🌸 Cultivate Communication

What are some of the themes of negative self-talk and larger negative narratives that you have told yourself over the years? Write them in your journal. Here are some examples of the negative thoughts you may experience:

- I'm fat.
- I'm too tall/short.
- I'm too old to . . .
- I'll never get that job.
- My nose is too big/small.
- I'm not good at . . .

For many of my clients, the larger narratives often begin with the words "should" or "shouldn't." For example:

- I shouldn't have . . . gotten a divorce.
- I shouldn't have . . . dropped out of college.
- I should have . . . taken that job.
- I should have . . . listened to my parents.
- He shouldn't have lied to me.
- She shouldn't have broken up with me.

Now go back and look at those stories and apply these questions: Is this thought or story true? Is it a balanced account of the facts, or do you sometimes exaggerate the details? Are there villains and victims in your story, or is everyone on equal footing? Is your story kind to you and others who make up the narrative? Is there another way you can view this story? What are some of the positives that occurred from it? Is there a way you can view your role and the role of others with kinder, gentler eyes?

Ultimately, Buddhism offers a way out of the stories that cause us suffering, and while a full discussion of that is beyond the scope of this book, the process begins with seeing them for what they are: simply stories. We will continue to work with these stories throughout this section, helping you to improve communication with yourself by learning how to spot and release the negative narratives. In the next section we will investigate how these stories generate feelings, as paying attention to your feelings is the second step in creating a new and positive communication model with yourself and others.

Pay Attention to Your Feelings

Feelings are hard for many of us to express, let alone tap into. Most of us have been taught to value our thoughts and practical, logical ways of being instead of our feelings. As our thoughts get looped together to become stories, and our stories become our beliefs, eventually we're so consumed by them that we stop acknowledging our feelings behind these stories.

Let's face it, feelings get a bad rap much of the time in our society. And as we saw in the last section, the thoughts in our head can be the product of others' influence. Not so with feelings; they are all felt individually. In other words, I can have the same thought as someone else, but I can't feel the feeling the exact same way someone else does. I might experience jealousy completely differently than you do. Or my sadness translates into crying, while yours might mean lying in the fetal position, holding yourself tight. Your feelings are unique to you; they are personal; they are yours.

Here's the thing, though. We pay more attention to our thoughts about ourselves than how we feel about ourselves. In order to really know our likes, dislikes, and needs in a given situation, and ultimately be able to express them rightly, we have to push aside the events and stories that have become overgrown, cutting them down to find ourselves again. Specifically, what we want to do is focus on our feelings and look past any negative self-talk and narratives that we've acquired over the years, seeing the stories for what they are: just stories. Breaking away, we are able to leave our heads and come into our hearts and feel the present moment. We are able to feel our pain and identify what we need to feel better. Without knowing how we feel, we can't know what we need; and if we don't know our needs, then we can't clearly express ourselves in a way that's kind, honest, and helpful. By focusing on our feelings instead of the stories in our head, we are able to delay our reactions in conversations to give us time to think about the next step and what the best action would be, instead of letting the stories and our automatic reactions to them do the thinking for us.

The Buddha taught that at its root, all human suffering is caused by two things: desire and fear. For the purposes of improving our communication skills, we will look at the role fear plays in negative self-talk, as most, if not all, of the feelings behind our stories are rooted in fear.

How we start to pay attention to our feelings is by first identifying the stories. Then we learn to look beyond the story so our feelings are revealed. Next, we will see if that feeling can be traced back to a fear.

Following are some common stories we tell ourselves and some of the feelings and fears that are hiding behind them.

Story	Potential Feelings	Underlying Fear
I'm too emotional.	Scared, lonely	People will hurt me if I expose myself.
I'm never getting that job.	Insecure, inadequate	I'm afraid of failing.
I'm too old for that.	Sad, discouraged, or depressed	I'm weak, boring, or "past my prime."
I'm fat.	Inadequate, insecure, despairing	I am not enough. I won't attract or keep a mate.
I'm a terrible friend/ daughter/wife/mother, father, son.	Guilt, shame	I wont be accepted by my family or community.
I'm not smart enough.	Inadequate, insecure, disappointed	I am not enough. I can't achieve my goals.
I should have stayed married.	Regretful, sad	I am "damaged" goods. I won't find "the one."
He/she shouldn't have lied to me.	Hurt, violated, righteous	I can't trust people, so I will keep to myself.
I should have taken that job.	Regretful, anxious, insecure	I won't have enough money in the future, or my career is off track.

Do you notice that the story and the fear column look very similar? As you can see, all of these stories ultimately create fear; they basically scream into our minds all that time: you aren't good enough; you are lacking in some way; you should be better than you are. Over and over again the stories push our fear buttons and then we doubt ourselves, adding more stories to the mix. This is a cyclical pattern. We get stuck in the story.

But our new action model for developing better communication with ourselves goes like this: Spot the story, see it as a story, and look for the feeling behind it. By acknowledging and processing the feeling, you can communicate with yourself better about your needs in the moment.

Detach from Your Stories, Focus on the Feeling

We can see how it's easy to get stuck on the merry-go-round of our minds. It's how we create much of our own pain. We step on it once and soon it's out of control, going around and around, too fast for us to jump off. Perhaps you can think about a handful of stories you regularly get caught up in. I can tell you from personal experience that it's a beautiful moment when you begin to notice yourself stuck in a story, because it's then you can choose not to believe it. To say to yourself, *This story isn't true. This isn't my story. I don't have to fall for this voice of lack.* The phrases are very basic but extremely powerful.

🏵Cultivate Communication

Close your eyes and think back to the last time you told yourself a story that was negative, or pick one of the stories you wrote down previously. Now say to yourself: *I don't have to believe this story. This story isn't true. This story isn't mine. This isn't the story I want to tell.*

Open your eyes and note how you feel. This is simply to show you how powerful those phrases are, and that saying this one phrase can break apart what before felt impossible to move through.

To detach from the story starts with noticing it and then reminding yourself not to get stuck in it; not to believe it. Doing this brings you into the present moment. It interrupts the thought pattern. It's here that you connect with how the story makes you feel, which can be hard, because in many cases our stories were created to prevent us from doing just this. Who really wants to feel sadness, shame, embarrassment, or disgust? But, yep, that's exactly what we need to do. And the more we stay in that uncomfortable space of being present with our feelings the more comfortable we become.

Close your eyes and come back to the story of lack. Get into that headspace again and tell yourself, *I don't have to believe this story. I'm not going to believe this story.* Then ask yourself, *What am I feeling when I believe this story? What is the pain I feel? What is the fear behind it? How am I hurting?* Open your eyes and note how you feel. There is something very transformative about releasing our stories and identifying our feelings and fears behind them, especially when we see that many of the fears we have are the result of our own making. Exposing these fears to the light of day begins to take away their power, because they are no longer unconsciously defining us.

So to recap, here's the process we have so far in this section:

Negative Story

⬇

I don't have to believe this story

⬇

What am I feeling right now?

⬇

Feel the feeling

⬇

We're paying attention now to our words and our feelings; now let's move into the last step of listening to ourselves: seeing ourselves with friendly eyes. After this next step, we'll put it all together and we'll have a different way of interacting with ourselves that helps us apply right speech not only with ourselves but also with others.

See Yourself with Friendly Eyes

Imagine for a moment that you're silently watching one of your closest friends as he goes about his day. And as you do, you notice that in certain situations he feels sad, insecure, inadequate, guilty, ashamed, anxious, and afraid. If you had the chance to speak to him in these instances, would you run up to him and start berating him? Would you tell him he isn't good enough? That he is weak and incapable? I doubt it. Yet, as you can see from the previous sections, this is exactly what many of us do to ourselves at various points throughout the day.

Buddhism teaches that this type of verbal self-flagellation is self-limiting and unnecessary on the bodhisattva's path to end suffering. I would go even further and say that this type of negative self-talk is suffering in and of itself. Going back to the analogy of witnessing a friend, what would you really say or do for him in his time of need? Like most of us, you would probably console him, encourage him, and do everything you could to help. In a word, you would be compassionate. So the third step in developing a new and healthy communication habit with yourself is to see yourself with the same friendly eyes, and to be compassionate toward yourself.

It may already be clear that much of the time we aren't practicing right speech by speaking to ourselves in a way that is true, balanced, kind, and helpful. We tell ourselves stories of lack, and if we aren't mindful we choose to believe them. But now we know that our thoughts and stories are simply thoughts and stories—and we don't have to believe them. This allows us to come into the present moment and identify the feelings that are causing the hurt inside. When we spot and feel the uncomfortable feeling, detached from the story, the next step is to wrap our arms around ourselves, look in the mirror, or close our eyes and say, *You're okay, you're good. You're safe in this moment. I believe in you.* We do this until calmed and ask the questions, *What can I do to make myself feel better? How can I be kind to myself in this moment? Through all this turbulence how can I even out? What do I need in this moment? What do I want in this moment?* What we're doing here is seeing the discomfort inside and saying to ourselves, *It's okay, I'm here for you. You're okay. I believe in you. Now what can we do about it?*

🏵️ Cultivate Communication

Close your eyes and come back to some of the negative self-talk and narratives you listed in the previous section. Get into that headspace again and tell yourself, *I don't have to believe this story. I'm not going to believe this story.* Then ask yourself, *What am I feeling when I think this way? What is the hurt I feel when I believe this story is true?* After you name the feeling, say to yourself, *I believe in you. You're okay. I accept the hurt I feel.* And when the moment comes when you accept the feeling, ask yourself, *What do I need to feel better? What would be the next step for me to help myself in this moment?*

Now here is what the process looks like:

Negative Story

I don't have to believe this story

What am I feeling right now?

Feel the feeling

What can I do to help myself feel better?

By putting these pieces together, we are now on the path to changing our internal communication style. Whereas before our speech came from a place of fear and lack, stuck in self-doubt and suffering, now we're transitioning into a kind, honest, judgment-free, and helpful response. When we release the negative self-talk and criticism around who we are, we see ourselves with clear and friendly eyes. Once we are no longer trapped by our own self-deprecating stories, we are better able to have conversations with others that are open, honest, and come with no agenda.

Cultivate Communication

Be mindful of your thoughts during the day, and when you hear yourself punishing or judging yourself through negative self-talk, try to identify the feeling behind it. Are you feeling insecure, ashamed, anxious, stressed, guilty, critical, or righteous? What is the fear behind it? What are you afraid of?

Remember, it's okay to be sad, to feel overwhelmed. Anything you are feeling is okay. The next question to ask yourself is, *How can I help myself feel better in this moment? What would I do without this thought?*

By listening to yourself, you can:

- Identify the thoughts and narratives that are causing you suffering.
- Detach from the story and feel the feelings behind them.
- Address the feeling instead of the story, giving yourself the comfort you would a dear friend in the same situation.

Notice if you begin to get mad at yourself for telling negative stories: *I can't believe I am still beating myself up for X, Y, or Z!* This is in itself another story. The subtlety of self-flagellation is amazing! In these instances stop and say, *I forgive you. You're human.* It may sound cheesy, but it does work.

Now that we've acquired the skills needed to talk to ourselves in an honest, kind, and useful way, we'll be taking a lot of these same techniques and applying them to how we speak to others.

Talking to Others

To listen to how we speak to others we'll be undertaking the same three steps as in the previous section, but the focus is now on paying attention to our interactions with others, not ourselves. From the steps below you can see the only change is in step 3, where our focus is on seeing compassion in others and ourselves.

1. Pay attention to your words and speech.

2. Pay attention to your feelings.

3. See others and yourself with friendly eyes.

Pay Attention to Your Words and Speech

When a habit emerges, the brain stops fully participating in decision making. It stops working so hard, or diverts focus to other tasks. So unless you deliberately fight a habit—unless you find new routines—the pattern will unfold automatically.

—Charles Duhigg

The Difference Between a Reaction and a Response

What most of my students find when they start observing their communication habits is that for much of the time they are on autopilot. In other words, they have adopted a communication routine, and when a situation arises they react in the same way they always do, generally without even thinking about it. In the context of communication, a response is very different than a reaction. Where a reaction is automatic, habitual, and arises out of your past conditioning, a response is mindful, balanced, and helpful. When you respond, you are aware of what's happening in the moment, including your past habits and your current feelings. A bodhisattva responds to the world, she doesn't react to it.

. . . .

🌸 Reacting versus Responding

People often ask what the difference is between reacting and responding. To react is instantaneous, without thought. To respond is gradual, with thought. What this five-step practice will teach you is how to move from a reaction that is not in line with the elements of right speech to a thoughtful response that follows the elements of right speech.

Before we can learn instead to respond, we first need to know what our habits of reacting are. When it comes to communicating with others, especially in conversations when we are triggered, what's our pattern? The more we notice our reactions, the easier it will be to redirect them. If we receive some constructive criticism at work, our initial reaction may be to berate the boss for being so stupid: *Who do they think they are? Why are they treating me like this?* Or maybe we shut down, thinking they're right, that we're just not a good employee. When we aren't mindful, we all have routine reactions, so it's time for you to find out what yours is.

How do you often react to stressful communication situations? By stressful, I mean a situation in which you feel uncomfortable, criticized, judged, or embarrassed. Do you:

- Lash out or attack—become aggressive, paranoid, blame others, feel frustrated that you put yourself through extremes, exaggerate, use hurtful language, believe in tit-for-tat?
- Dodge—justify your behavior, make up excuses, lie, deny responsibility, have a reason for everything, have to explain yourself?
- Shut down—go into your own world, get quiet and depressed, feel lost or confused, feel so overwhelmed that you have to leave the situation, do what someone else asks instead of what you want, avoid conflict at all cost—even if it means sacrificing your own truth in the process?

- Lie—say everything is fine when it isn't or pretend to agree when really you don't, end up feeling resentful, and maybe even plot revenge?
- Take things personally—all you hear when someone disagrees with you is blame and criticism, and you get defensive and become the victim, taking the judgment and wearing it like an outfit?
- Make assumptions—presume that because someone doesn't like one aspect of what you are doing that he or she doesn't like the whole thing; assume the worst?
- Stop listening—dismiss others' criticism as having little or no value; you know better, so you don't need to hear what they have to say?

. . . .

🌸 Cultivate Communication

Much like when you listen to yourself, the first step is to notice any unhealthy habits you currently have when it comes to listening to how you speak to others. Think about the stressful communication situations you've been in over the last few months, when you have done any of the above. In your journal, write down specific instances when you have reacted rather than responded. Why do you think you are receiving information in this way? When you lash out, shut down, take things personally, or make assumptions, do you do so because you feel less than, unworthy, or not deserving of goodness? Or maybe you have the opposite reaction. Do you tend to dodge or dismiss others' comments as unmerited without investigating them first?

Identifying our automatic reactions to stressful communication situations is important so that we can see it happening in the moment and course correct. Take a few minutes to identify how you receive information. More than one of these descriptions may apply to you, depending on the situation or the relationship. For example, are you more likely to make assumptions or shut down when in a discussion with your boss? Are you more dismissive of criticism from your friends or children?

Only when we become aware of how we react to situations can we find out what we need to change within ourselves in order to respond. Remember, our goal is to communicate with others in a kind, honest, judgment-free, and helpful way. Let's take a look at an example of the difference between a reaction and a response.

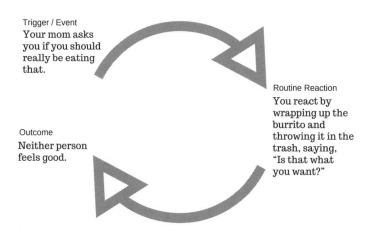

Trigger / Event
Your mom asks you if you should really be eating that.

Routine Reaction
You react by wrapping up the burrito and throwing it in the trash, saying, "Is that what you want?"

Outcome
Neither person feels good.

The above scenario illustrates an automatic reaction. Maybe you feel like you're being judged or criticized, so you react in this way. Think about how this reaction feeds the outcome. Now look at the following.

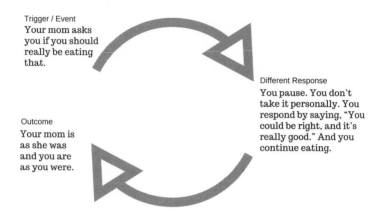

Trigger / Event
Your mom asks you if you should really be eating that.

Different Response
You pause. You don't take it personally. You respond by saying, "You could be right, and it's really good." And you continue eating.

Outcome
Your mom is as she was and you are as you were.

The change in the above scenario is in the response and the outcome. And by changing the response, we get another kind of outcome. Basically, we can't avoid stressful situations, and we will often have different opinions than others. While we can't change others' feelings or actions (nor, in most cases, should we want to), we can change how we respond to them, making the interaction either helpful or at least less painful for all parties involved. So how do we change our automatic reactions into thoughtful responses? By paying attention to our feelings and taking responsibility for them.

Pay Attention to Your Feelings

It's the classic exchange between couples that you see on television all the time. The guy comes home late and immediately sees a look of irritation on his partner's face. "What's wrong?" he asks. "Nothing," she replies. "Really? What's wrong?" "Nothing."

Whenever I see this on TV or in movies, I want to jump into the conversation and whisper in the partner's ear, "It's not nothing. What you're feeling is not nothing. It's something. And you can do something about it." I get a bit worked up around this back and forth because I've been there. I've kept my true feelings inside as a form of punishment for my partner not being able to read my mind. I've kept my feelings inside because I didn't really know what I was feeling in the first place. I've kept my feelings inside because I didn't trust my own perspective. It's the lack of trust in our emotions and the attachment to story that keeps us from expressing ourselves honestly, without exaggeration, manipulation, or negativity. In this scenario, the response of "nothing" is a form of shutting down and lying.

The "nothing" is a direct response to the event of being late—the word and intonation implies that something is wrong even though the woman is saying that nothing is. There's no tapping into the feeling of what her partner showing up late makes her feel; no expression of the hurt so something can be done about it. In many cases like this, what are often there instead are thoughts whirling around such as, *How can he not understand why I'm upset right now? I shouldn't even have to say anything. And I can't believe he's late again.* If this has happened multiple times without being expressed, what's happening in her head may even be more hurtful: *What an asshole he is. I hate him sometimes. He really doesn't take me into consideration at all; he's so selfish.*

We can see here that the woman's attention is caught in the story, and instead of focusing on her feelings and ultimately speaking her truth, she fell back into an automatic reaction. Do you think this leads to a healthy dialogue, to expression that's honest, equal, free of judgment, and helpful? Likely not, because if we ignore how we feel and get stuck in the internal thoughts and story then we keep the merry-go-round spinning; we're keeping ourselves in a situation that can't change. What if she had actually listened to her partner and responded accurately when he asked, "What's wrong?"

If instead of falling into an old story and habit, perhaps she could have mindfully shifted to the present moment and the feeling she was feeling when he asked. If she pauses to look within herself to see how she's feeling, there is a delay in her response, a pause; in that moment she'd no longer be consumed by the story. She would come into herself and ask, *How do I feel right now? How does this action make me feel?* By taking the focus off what can't change (the fact that he is late) she begins to focus on what can (how she expresses how she feels about it). And by coming into the present moment and focusing on her feelings she gives herself the time needed to choose another response, to take responsibility for her feelings.

Like we did in the previous section on listening to how we speak to ourselves, we shift our focus to what we're feeling rather than reverting to an unhealthy habit. Now let's move on to the final step, which is just as important here as it was in the previous section.

Seeing Others and Ourselves With Friendly Eyes

When we're in tense situations, it's easy to fall into old habits; we're not aware of our words or feelings and instead get stuck in reactive mode: "Yes you did." "No I didn't." "You did." "I didn't." You get the picture. Conversations like these are reactive, and the result is that we often feel bad about what was said and nothing is really resolved.

But once we start applying the first two steps when we communicate with others, we're more than halfway there to having tools in place to respond rather than react. The third step, practicing compassion toward others and yourself, is the next piece needed to be able to apply the elements of right speech in our conversations, especially when things start to get stressful.

Let's keep with the previous example, apply the first two steps, and then we can go one step further. The woman's partner has come home late. She notes the event, is mindful of her previous habits around issues like this, and when he asks, "What's wrong?" she comes in to focus on what she is feeling in the present moment. She closes her eyes and says to herself, *It's okay. You're okay. How are you feeling?*

Perhaps she feels angry, hurt, disappointed, or anxious. Next, she identifies what the fear is behind the feeling:

- He's late, and I am angry. I'm afraid we won't have time to do the things I had planned.
- He's late, and I am hurt or disappointed. I'm afraid he doesn't value me and my time, as he thinks it's okay not to keep commitments to me.
- He's late, and I am anxious. I'm afraid he is out with someone else.
- Are these just stories I'm telling myself? What would this situation look like without the stories?

Next, she sees herself through the eyes of compassion and asks herself what she needs to feel better. And since this is an interaction with another as opposed to just herself, she remembers to see the other person with compassion too. Once the fear is realized and acknowledged, she can see that the fear is hers, not his. When she sees this, she can see that he isn't trying to hurt her by being late. He isn't intentionally trying to make her suffer. Seeing this makes compassion for the other possible.

Another tool you can use to help you get to a place of compassion is to see if what you are feeling about the current situation is actually something triggered from your past. In this example, perhaps the woman was in a previous relationship in which her partner consistently came home late and she later found out it was because he was cheating on her. If that were the case, she could be mindful of her previous experience, and how this could lead her to project the fears of the past on to her current relationship. Mindfully, she can now see that this fear originated in circumstances that have nothing to do with her current partner. Recognizing this would allow her to see her current partner with compassionate eyes.

Compassion enters our communication the moment we begin to see where the other person is coming from. The other person now becomes an equal participant instead of an opposing force we need to deal with. And it's in these instances, when we know the other person isn't trying to hurt us or make us feel the way we do, that we are ready to ask ourselves what we need to feel better, and we can be mindful if there is anything we can do to be helpful to the other person. Once we have identified both, we are ready to speak in a way that is honest, equal, nonjudgmental, and helpful.

One caveat: I want to be clear that compassion does not mean we become a doormat. Compassion can also be there when we have to tell someone good-bye because his or her behavior is no longer acceptable.

Here is the process for noticing how we speak to others:

Stressful Situation

⬇

I choose not to get stuck in the incident/story.

⬇

I focus on the present moment. The feeling I feel.

⬇

I'm okay. I'm good. I believe in me.

⬇

When was the first time I felt this feeling?

⬇

See with compassion.

⬇

How can I make myself feel better?
How can I make this interaction helpful?

One of the most important pieces in transforming your communication from reactive to responsive is to simply pause before speaking. Why? Because this is where you get the opportunity to reflect on how you are feeling in the present moment, see yourself and others with compassion, and in so doing, you are far more likely to move away from reacting in the same old way.

Incidentally, the examples so far have focused on the

spoken word as the means of communication, but these tools can also be applied to the written word, which is especially useful in the modern world where e-mail, texting, and social media make up much of our communication.

For example, I recently e-mailed a document for a project at work to someone, and he responded immediately by saying he wished that I had done more work on it. My initial reaction was to defend why I hadn't done more, and to say that this was never something we agreed on. What he was asking me to do was his job, in my reactive opinion. Then I paused, came into the present moment, and felt that feeling of irritation. In doing so, I was able to look past the current exchange and identify a situation where I'd felt this feeling before. Once I made this realization, I knew that this person wasn't intentionally trying to hurt me, and I could see him with friendly eyes again. Then I thought of his desire. What was he needing? Where was he coming from? Although he could have worded his response differently, I knew he wasn't trying to attack or criticize. At that point, I thought about what I needed in the situation and what I could offer him. Only then, once I could see the situation calmly and clearly, was I able to respond.

Sometimes with e-mails it can be easier, because you don't have to respond right away. But I'd like to advocate the idea that you can pause a conversation as well. For example, let's say you are in a conversation and you get caught somewhere between these steps—you've identified your feelings but can't get to a place of compassion. I suggest saying something like, "I really want to discuss this, but I think things are a bit confusing and complicated for me right now. I need some time to think about this and get back to you."

E-mails, texting, and social media can also make communication more difficult, as brevity can make it harder to express yourself fully, and it leaves things open to interpretation. When you're writing to someone, be mindful of the habit of "filling in the blanks," aka making assumptions. Most of us have heard stories or been involved in e-mail exchanges that went awry in this fashion. When you sense that may be a possibility, I suggest stating, "Let's put this discussion off until we can talk face-to-face. I want to make sure we understand each other fully."

Can I See the Humor in This?

One often overlooked tool that can help us communicate more effectively is humor, which, much like the pause, can help defuse tension in a stressful situation. Many people equate Buddhism with constantly being serious, but that's not the case. The following Zen story illustrates this perfectly:

> A young Zen student was given the job of arranging flowers for the various altars in the temple. He was a very serious sort of young man and was concerned about doing a proper job. There may also have been a bit of vanity involved. "Flowers no higher than the statue's eye. Check. Odd number of flowers in the vase. Check. No thorns or spiky flowers. Check. No all-white arrangements except for funerals. Check." As he was working, an older monk came into the room, watched for a moment and asked, "Do you want to know how to make a perfect arrangement for the altar?" "Oh, yes!" said the youngster. "Well,"

said the monk, "You take a bunch of flowers, put them in a vase, step back and say 'That's perfect!'"[1]

One lesson of this story is to remember not to take yourself too seriously. We can get stuck in our stories, but can we find the humor in them? I make it a goal to laugh every day (at myself and with others). When something unexpected happens, I ask myself, can I laugh at this? In situations when you've maybe told your boss over and over again that the client is on vacation and then seconds later he asks you where the client is; when you call your sister to tell her good news and the first words out of her mouth are hold on; or when you turn the coffee pot on without any coffee in it. All those instances could set you off, but what if instead you laughed it off? There's a card I read a while ago that says if your boyfriend is angry and you put an imaginary cape around him and say, "Ta-da! Now you're super angry!" and he laughs, marry him.

Being able to make fun of ourselves, laugh at our actions, and not take ourselves so seriously means we are detaching from the dramatic story that involves seeing ourselves as the victor or victim. Being able to find the humor in conversations that could potentially turn sour can make an overwhelming situation more manageable, easier to talk through and re-evaluate.

So why is laughter so great at defusing tense situations? Because it brings us back to the present moment. Think about the last time you had a laughing attack. Were you thinking about anything else besides laughing? It's when we're laughing that we redirect our initial frustration and

---

1 This story appears in a free publication of the San Francisco Zen Center, *Teachings from Meditation in Recovery: Prajna Paramita, The Perfection of Wisdom.*

see things from a different perspective. It opens the space around the problem we're facing, making it easier to handle. It's hard to feel annoyed or angry if you're laughing. It's hard to feel disappointed or rejected if you're laughing, and it's hard to be sad and afraid if you're laughing. Laughing relaxes us, lets us be okay in the moment, and that improves our communication. It gives us the opportunity to accept the situation and to let go of judgment and criticism. As we do all of this, we not only improve our relationship with ourselves but also with those around us.

Learning to listen to the way you speak to yourself and others is essential for creating a new communication routine. By listening you give yourself the opportunity to break free from old patterns of reacting and open the way for conversations that are kind, honest, and helpful.

What to Remember

- How to listen to yourself: pay attention to your words, identify how you feel, and see yourself and others with friendly eyes.
- How to detach from stories: see the story as a story, and remember that you don't have to believe it. Come into the present moment by focusing on how you feel and determine what you truly need to feel better instead of focusing on what is wrong with the other person or the event that's activating the feeling inside you.
- Process of responding: observe the want to automatically react, pause, identify the feeling associated with the initial reaction (have you

felt this before?), see yourself and the other person with compassion, and identify what you can do to make yourself feel better. Put it together in a sentence: action + feeling + what you need to feel better.

Listen to Others

Do not let the behavior of others destroy your inner peace.

—Dalai Lama

Maybe this has happened to you. Your phone rings. You pick it up. And suddenly there's a man or woman on the other end talking to you about renewing a subscription, or making a donation, or supporting a political candidate. Sometimes they can go on for five minutes before you have the opportunity to speak. How many times do you think this person is allowed to get through their whole spiel? And how many of these conversations leave both parties feeling satisfied? I would say, in the grand scheme of things, this approach probably doesn't get too many wins. Why? Because the minute we identify a salesperson on the line, we shut down. It doesn't matter what they have to say; all we want is to get off the phone fast. We interrupt. We talk over them, thinking that our needs and our time are more important, which gives us permission to disregard what they're saying.

Well, what if I told you that this kind of communication cycle happens in lots of different situations every day? Whether we know it or not, we treat a lot of people, most of the time the ones closest to us, like that salesperson. Think back to the last time you stopped listening to someone else. Maybe you took something they said personally so you checked out; you thought you knew what they were going to say so you stopped paying attention and pretended you were listening by nodding along. Based on what we've learned, behavior like this creates an environment that nurtures automatic reactions instead of responses that are conducive to the elements of right speech. Our goal is to create an environment where kind, honest, and helpful speech can take place, and learning how to listen to others is an important step toward that aim.

To learn how to listen to others we'll be undertaking four steps:

1. Be present.

2. See things from the other person's point of view.

3. Learn to accept what's true.

4. Ask yourself if there is a way you can help.

If we were to apply the above techniques to the salesperson example, instead of interrupting, we would be in the present moment, completely focused on the call instead of involved in our thoughts of why we don't have time for this or what we have to do immediately afterward. We would understand that the person is doing her job and that her performance is likely being evaluated, and accept that at first we were being led by our own agenda. Then we'd ask ourselves, *How can I help this person?* By letting her be heard and telling her honestly whether we can or can't commit to what she's offering. Applying these four steps will turn us away from our automatic reactions and into impeccable listeners who then respond in a way that's kind, honest, and helpful.

How to Listen to Others

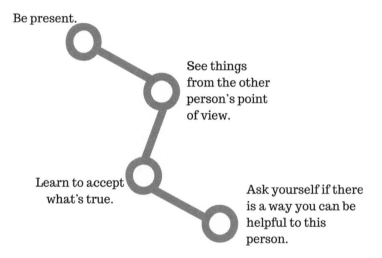

Be present.

See things from the other person's point of view.

Learn to accept what's true.

Ask yourself if there is a way you can be helpful to this person.

Be Present

The other day I taught a class, and while listening to one of my students I noted that I wasn't paying attention. While he read his story, my mind wandered. I thought about the amount of time left in the class and if I had enough material to fill the workshop. As he read his last sentence, I realized I had no idea what his work was about.

When we're not listening, our minds move here and there. We judge what we hear, think about what we want to say next, or how what the other person is saying relates to our own lives instead of trying to understand how they feel. When we're not listening, we're more irritable with the person who is talking, because we want them to wrap it up so we can get back to what we're doing, thinking, or saying. But if we are present with them and move our attention out of our heads and into the moment, we give others the opportunity to be heard and ourselves the opportunity to help them.

. . . .

🌸 Cultivate Communication

Think about a time when someone wasn't listening to you. What did he or she do to make you feel that way? Maybe he or she was closed off, placated you, reacted instead of responded. How did you feel? What about the last time you remember not listening? What were you thinking or doing instead? The more aware you are of the ways you close yourself off from listening, the easier these actions are to spot while you're in a conversation. Simply note them without judgment and come back to the present moment.

When we're present we're living in the moment. Our attention is focused on whatever is in front of us, without any distractions, and from here we can listen to another person's words. What we learn by practicing presence is that we'll go in and out of it, and when we notice that our minds have wandered off into what we are doing in the next hour, day, or week, we gently turn our attention around and step back into the now. Being present in the moment is a central component of communicating like a Buddhist, as you can only practice the elements of right speech now, not at some point in the future.

So how do you become a present listener? By decluttering your headspace before a conversation begins, noticing when your mind wanders, and then gently guiding yourself back to the moment you're in without judgment—again, and again, and again.

How to Be a Present Listener

Before a conversation: Declutter your headspace.

During a conversation: Notice the moment you're in.

Before a Conversation: Declutter Your Headspace

There's a scene in the movie *Singles* in which Campbell Scott, one of the stars of the movie, sits in front of his bosses to pitch a project. He's consumed by a recent breakup, though, and his mind is elsewhere. There's a shot of his bosses talking, but all we hear is the inner dialogue going on in Scott's head.

This is similar to how a lot of us live every day. And the more aware we are of the stories and thoughts in our minds that prevent us from listening to others, the easier they'll be to spot as they come up. It's in this noticing of our usual distractions that we can start to implement some techniques to declutter our minds. I offer three techniques you can use to clear the clutter from your mind and focus on the present. These are in no particular order, and I encourage you to try all three and see which work best for you.

Breathe Until the Clutter Clears

Let's say you are about to meet a friend for a conversation, or you're getting ready to go into a meeting, speak with someone on the phone, or even just sit down for dinner with family or a date. A good way to clear the clutter so you're present for the interaction is to find a place to sit quietly for a moment (sometimes it's the bathroom!), close your eyes, and scan your body from head to toe, noticing any areas that feel tight or uncomfortable. Connecting to your body is a great way to center yourself in the present moment. Next, breathe in and imagine the air coming into your entire body, and as you breathe out imagine this air whisking away any area that feels constricted, including any stressful thoughts or bottled-up emotions. Keep inhaling and exhaling slowly until you feel clean and clear. Where before there was no room, now you feel spaciousness, and your head and heart are ready to pay attention to the moment you're in.

Try this practice and note how much more open you feel, and how well you are able to be present in the conversation.

Name What You're Grateful For

Sometimes I think of our minds as storage units. We've placed things in there over time and left them, rarely, if ever, going back to take another look to see if we still need what we left or if we would be better off throwing them away. Too much mental stuff can create a feeling of heaviness if we don't take the time to clean out our internal space.

This may surprise you, but one effective way to declutter our headspace and detach from our storage units of the past is to be grateful for what we have today. That's because gratitude brings us into the present moment, and the things we are grateful for replace any mental baggage we are holding on to that is simply taking up space.

🏵 Cultivate Communication

Gratitude Exercise 1

Take a minute to think of all that you are grateful for in your life. When I do this I think about my health: my legs for taking me where I need to go, my arms, my hands. I think about my family, friends. The sun. The sky. By saying to ourselves what we're grateful for, we come into the present moment, notice our surroundings, and be with what it is we truly cherish. One I love to say is, "I'm grateful for this moment." It brings me immediately into the present. When we're consciously grateful for what we have, we are unpacking our minds of anything negative that is taking up space, replacing them with thoughts of gratitude. When we are grateful for what we have, we project that gratitude in our interactions with others.

Gratitude Exercise 2

Take ten to fifteen minutes every morning and write down five or ten things you are grateful for. Once you are done, read that list *out loud* to yourself, with emotion, so your body feels and hears the gratitude in your voice. Do this every day for thirty days and notice if you feel more grounded, present, and attentive in your everyday interactions.

Gratitude Exercise 3

Think of the week ahead and someone you'll be interacting with at work or in your personal life that you have previously had a hard time listening to or being attentive with. Then, on a sheet of paper write down the following phrase:

I am grateful for [insert name] because . . .

List four or five things about them that you are grateful for. In the morning, or before you interact with the person, read these proclamations out loud. Finally, remember these statements of gratitude just before, making you an attentive listener.

Write the Clutter Down

The last way to declutter your mind before a conversation is very practical, as much of the clutter that occupies our minds consists of things we need to do throughout the day. Things like dropping off the dry cleaning, going to the bank, picking up the kids, calling Mom, finishing that project at work, etc. When we have so many to-do tasks running in our heads, it's no wonder we have trouble being present in the moment, sitting still and silent, being attentive to someone else.

One way to get those things out of your mind is to set aside a few minutes each day and put them on paper. Some of my clients prefer to make a list every night of what they need to get done the following day, and it actually helps them sleep better too. Others prefer to make a list of the day ahead in the morning. Either can work. The point here is that by making a list of the tasks you know you need to get done, you no longer need to think or worry about them as you go throughout your day, interacting with others. Writing them down gets them out of your head and onto the page, which gives them another place to live instead of inside your mind. You can then set specific times to refer back to your list throughout the day and check off what's done, or plan to do what isn't. When we write down our to-do list, we help empty our minds so we can be clear and attentive with the moment we're in.

. . . .

🌸 Cultivate Communication

For one week, I invite you to write down your to-do list for the day either the night before or early in the morning before you start your day. Get all the "I need to call . . ." or "I have to pick up . . ." tasks down on the page. Next, set specific times throughout the day to check your list and see what can be marked off or still needs to be done, remind yourself that you don't need to think about these things in between check-ins. The more you get what's distracting you on the page, the easier it will be for you to be there in conversations and effectively listen to the people you're with.

Now that we have covered some things you can do to help yourself be present in conversations before these interactions take place, let's explore ways to be present and attentive during a conversation.

During a Conversation: Notice the Moment You're In

When you're in a conversation, notice when you drift into thoughts of what you're doing later that evening, or what happened earlier that day—basically anything other than what's happening in the here and now. In the modern technological world, this also includes checking your phone during a conversation, as this is another attempt to take yourself away from the present.

Another subtle trap that can pull you away from listening to others is thinking about what you're going to say next instead of really listening to what the other person has to say. This can fool you, because you may still think you are in the present moment. But there is a difference between hearing and listening, as listening requires your full, undivided attention.

When you become aware that you have drifted, simply acknowledge that to yourself without judgment and bring your attention back into the present interaction. The great thing is that we can always start fresh. We can always say, "Excuse me, could you repeat that?" or "Let me make sure I understand you correctly," or "This is what I'm hearing you say, is that correct?" and repeat back to the person what you think you heard. Something I do a lot is silently say, *I'm here right now. How do I want to be present for this moment? For this person? For this interaction?*

The other week, I had a student who was going through a lot emotionally. She was having a hard time expressing herself and was holding in so much. I wanted to help her, but I could tell by our conversation that she wasn't ready yet for any feedback, and that's okay too, as we can't listen until we're ready to. I was conscious to listen only, be present, and not make any plan for what I needed to say next.

After class, Bryan picked me up. We drove to the grocery store, and I couldn't get the student out of my head as we were shopping. He was asking me questions but I wasn't paying attention. I was thinking more about the girl in class, hoping that she was feeling better. Standing between the broccoli and me, Bryan put his hands on my shoulders and said, "We're in the grocery store now. Whatever happened in class, let it go. We're here now." I looked into his eyes. He was right. This was a new moment I wanted to be present for. I noted the feeling in my body and let it dissipate. *I'm here now,* I said to myself. *This is a new moment. Be here now.* We're always noticing, detaching, noticing, detaching. Being present is a constant state of refocusing on the moment at hand.

Being present during a conversation looks like the following:

Process of Being Present in a Conversation

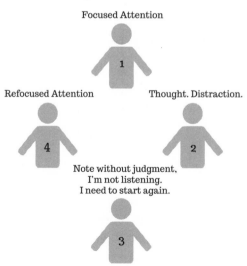

Focused Attention

1

Refocused Attention

Thought. Distraction.

4

2

Note without judgment,
I'm not listening.
I need to start again.

3

Another important part of refocusing our attention is not to get upset with ourselves or beat ourselves up for having drifted off into another stream of thought. To do so would create another negative story line: "I'm such a bad listener!" This takes us out of the moment and prevents us from being helpful. Instead, when you catch yourself drifting, simply notice you have drifted and begin listening again, without judgment.

The more we tame the mind's habit to wander and get lost in thoughts and other distractions (including our own negative stories and judgments), the more present our interactions will become. When you become fully present in conversations, people notice. Don't be surprised when you begin to hear comments like, "You're such a good listener," or "I can really talk to you." Being present in the moment creates fertile ground for real communication to germinate and grow.

🌸 Cultivate Communication

Here's a creative way you can remind yourself to come back to the present moment. Wear a rubber band, a bracelet, or a ring you like—anything that you can see easily—and when you notice that band, bracelet, or ring during a conversation, say to yourself, *I'm here now. I'm in this moment.* Take a breath. Notice the person in front of you and come back to him or her. Let this item serve as a natural reminder to come back to the present moment. We meander for a minute, note our attention is somewhere else, and then we come back.

By drifting and refocusing, we're constantly coming back to the present moment again and again, keeping us tied to the conversation we're in and aware of its needs. Being present is the first piece we need in place to listen effectively. The second is being able to see things from the other person's point of view.

See Things from the Other Person's Point of View

I recently had a client whose husband traveled a lot for work. For the majority of each week, he was away and she was at home taking care of their two daughters. Over time, she found a routine for the girls that made the days and nights alone much more manageable and also helped her feel calm and capable doing things on her own. But oftentimes when her husband arrived home on Friday nights, he'd alter that routine and the girls would get wound up, out of sync, and this lasted for the weekend. Then on Monday she'd have to apply the rules all over again. As a result, the very limited time they had together was spent fighting over his actions and her reactions.

Fortunately, the arguing stopped. Why? Because they both took a minute to see the situation from the other person's point of view. He thought about how she would spend the entire week implementing a schedule that was working well for the girls, and how he'd come in like a whirling dervish and mess it up. By seeing it from her perspective, he realized how she could feel disrespected by his actions. She saw that he'd been working hard away from his wife and kids all week long, and that all he wanted was to come home and be playful with the girls, showering them with love and enjoying every moment he could with them while he was home, including letting them stay up late.

Once they saw each other's perspectives, they were able to have a dialogue that was kind, honest, and helpful. Seeing from the other person's perspective delays our automatic reactions, giving us time and space to choose how to respond. It's in that space that we alleviate the back-and-forth automatic reactions.

The act of seeing from another person's perspective can be difficult, but it's impossible to do so if we aren't even trying. We can get so caught up in our automatic reactions of defending, attacking, or shutting down that we forget to practice kindness and compassion. Our minds are often quick to judge, but by seeing things from the other person's perspective we can better understand the words for what they are—an expression of what the person is experiencing or has experienced in the past. When we can see this, we can see his or her actions as a reflection of who he or she is and not take them personally. The truth is it's never personal—even when it's intended to be.

How, then, do you learn to see from another person's perspective? By shifting focus away from I, me, and my, thinking of others' unique experiences, and then asking yourself if there's a way you can see this situation differently.

How to See from Another Person's Perspective

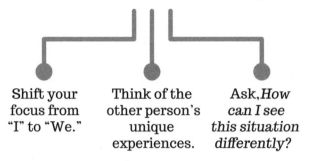

| Shift your focus from "I" to "We." | Think of the other person's unique experiences. | Ask, *How can I see this situation differently?* |

Shift Your Focus from "I" to "We"

We live our lives from the first person perspective. But just because it's the only point of view we know doesn't mean we're the only ones experiencing the highs and lows. To see another person's point of view is an act of compassion, and in doing so we realize that we're not the only one who is experiencing loss or heartache, who is busy and tired after a long day, or who is feeling any one of the other innumerable forms of suffering that occur in everyday life. Remember, we all want the same thing: to be happy, to be understood, and to avoid suffering.

Imagine that every person on the planet is an egg walking around with a cracked shell, with hurt and joy pouring out like lava. This is really how we all go through life: cracked, flawed, and wanting the same things—to be seen, heard, and loved. To see from another person's perspective we must view him or her as an equal. We must be willing to let go of our own agendas; strip ourselves of our obsessions with I, me, and my, and instead think of we. When we enter a conversation viewing everyone involved as deserving of love and support, we are in a position to listen to their experiences and look at the current situation differently.

. . . .

✹ Cultivate Communication

For one day, try not to respond to someone using "I," "me," or "my" in a conversation. For those of you who haven't done this you may be surprised how difficult it is. In general, refraining from using I, me, and my and being mindful of when you do will help you shift away from a "me only" perspective and move into an awareness of others.

Think of Others' Unique Experiences

In the first chapter I mentioned my best friend who passed away, and how his death set me on the road to where I am today. What I didn't mention was that he was also my first love. We met when we were eighteen during our freshman year of college. I was from Ohio. He was from Costa Rica. As you can imagine, we came from two different worlds.

At that time, though, I rarely thought outside of my own frame of reference. Instead, I believed that he, and pretty much everyone else my age, had either the same or similar experiences as me growing up, and of course that wasn't true. But because that was my belief, I had a hard time understanding why he would tell me that he loved me but was so scared to commit to me, or why the minute things were good between us he would often do something to sabotage them.

We were together for a total of seven and a half years, and almost every fight we had centered on these issues. In hindsight, I know now that his parents' divorce when he was younger had an impact on his actions and reactions. But I couldn't see that then. Although he tried desperately to get me to see where he was coming from, I ignored it, choosing not to believe him because I was so caught up in my own experiences and stories. Today, knowing that to understand someone's actions I need to understand their unique experiences, I can see why he did the things he did.

While we all want the same things, we haven't all had the same experiences. That being said, there are some things we all have in common: we have all experienced loss, suffering, and even tragedy at some point in our lives. So when you are in a conversation, especially one that has the potential to get tense or uncomfortable, I invite you to think of what pain the other person has gone through. While you may not know the details, you can be sure that this person has experienced his or her own share of heartache, loss, insecurity, and fear. How do I know this? Because we all have. It's the human condition. With this in mind, you can be mindful of how the person's past experiences could influence speech and social interactions. By remembering this, it's much easier to practice compassion for the other person, as well as listening more intently, as every single person has something unique to tell you. When you really listen, you are now in a position to see a situation from another's perspective.

🌸 Cultivate Communication

In your journal, write down people in your life whom you have had a hard time listening to in the past, or have a hard time listening to in your current relationship. Next to their names, write down what their lives might have been like growing up, what you imagine they've gone through, and what experiences may have affected their perception of the world. If you don't have enough information to make these guesses, write this instead:

This person has known suffering and now wishes to feel love.

This person has known suffering and now wishes to be happy.

This person has known suffering and now wishes to feel seen.

This person has known suffering and now wishes to be heard.

Notice if this exercise changes your perspective about these people. Can you feel their hurt? Can you feel their desire? Can you see their humanness? Where before your perception was perhaps closed, can you feel a slight opening? Notice if you are better able to listen the next time you communicate with these individuals.

Try to See the Situation from Another Perspective

One of my communication clients, Jill, has been with the same company for over twenty years. Recently, her boss hired a couple of new employees right out of college and tasked them with helping introduce the company's product to a younger market. Jill noticed in meetings with these new coworkers that she was more combative than usual, and quick to say things like, "Well, we can't do that because . . ." or "Our customers will never go for that . . ." What's more, she also noticed that her reactions sparked a reaction from the new employees, as they would fire back with comments like, "Well, sure, that may have worked fifteen years ago . . ." or "If you knew what people were looking at these days, you would . . ." As you might imagine, little progress was being made in formulating her boss's plan to reach new customers.

Jill really wanted the best for the situation, and that included her boss, her coworkers, and the company's customers, so during our session I asked her the following questions: How can you see this situation differently? Can you see this from the perspective of your new coworkers? Is there anything you are afraid of here?

Looking within, she noticed right away that she felt threatened by these new employees. At the same time, she also knew that many of the ideas they were presenting were typical of people not familiar with her industry, and would likely not be well received by their customers. Jill had to find the balance between her fear (not helpful) and her experience (helpful), and until that moment her fear had been getting the best of her.

As a result of looking at the situation again, she began to see things differently. We decided that speaking to her colleagues about their previous conversations or her internal realizations wasn't necessary, and instead a change in her communication style when dealing with them would likely produce the desired result.

Before the next meeting, Jill made it a point to take a few minutes at her desk and do the breathing exercise described on page 82. As a result, she went into the meeting more calm and centered and was mindful to be in the present moment, attentively listening to the ideas of the other attendees.

Shifting her perspective from I to We, she thought about how they all wanted the same thing: to help more customers and the company by getting more of their products into the market. She imagined the perspective of her new coworkers and remembered what it was like for her when she started a brand-new job.

By putting these steps into action, Jill was able to listen to her coworkers' ideas in a new way, and when it was her turn to respond she was careful to choose words that would most likely be interpreted as helpful. Doing all of these things created an open and equal space for everyone to share, and I am pleased to report that Jill now has an excellent working relationship with her colleagues.

When we can see a situation from another's perspective, then we know we are letting go of the I, Me, and My perception, and in so doing, we are better able to tap into the collective desire of all parties involved.

Seeing from the other person's perspective doesn't mean that we're giving in, or that we're disregarding our own thoughts and feelings, as there's a difference between giving up our position and understanding where the other person is coming from. By seeing from the other person's perspective, we're acknowledging the other as an equal; therefore, neither one voice nor the other is dominant.

Even in situations when an agreement cannot be

reached, when the other person realizes that you are honestly attempting to see things from his or her perspective it can make all the difference between a conversation that feels productive and one that does not.

🌸 Cultivate Communication

Following are some all-too-common phrases that signal to the other person that you aren't genuinely seeing things from his or her perspective:

- "You shouldn't feel that way."
- "I wouldn't feel that way if I were you."
- "That's not what happened—you're getting it all wrong."
- "That's so ridiculous."
- "I have no clue what you're talking about."

Here are some phrases that can indicate you are seeing things from another's perspective. Try incorporating some of these in your next conversation:

- "I hear what you are saying and I understand."
- "I see what you mean."
- "Thank you for sharing that with me."
- "I'm so glad you told me how you feel about this."
- "I'm glad you explained your position to me. That's helpful."
- "I've never thought about it that way before."

Learn to Accept What's True

One of the hardest parts about listening to others is when they tell us things about ourselves that we don't like but ultimately recognize are true. If I interrupt somebody and it's pointed out by saying something like, "Can you let me finish?" it can take all my strength to keep from reacting. Just the other day I was having a conversation with a friend when she said, "Why are you getting so defensive?" I could feel the heat rising in my body. If I had opened my mouth right away, I'm certain fire would have soared out and burnt off her eyebrows.

When you feel yourself react like this to criticism, it's a good indication that the criticism is true—at least on some level. The practice of listening to others invites us to look within, and accept any truth that we find. Constructive feedback is actually a gift, some piece of information about yourself that you have hitherto been unable to see, but you have to make yourself willing and available to receive it.

For example, when someone tells me something about myself that I don't like, the hair stands up on the back of my neck. I take that as my cue that I really need to listen. I've found that if I don't, then my defense mechanisms take over, and instead of seeing the truth and not exaggerating, gossiping, or using harsh language, I will employ the opposite of all four elements of right speech, often without even noticing I'm doing it.

But here is the good news: the moment you acknowledge the truth and say, "You're right, I said something hurtful," or "You're right, I'm acting selfishly right now," you defuse any defense mechanism. By admitting the truth, we free ourselves and our conversations.

Sometimes we may feel some discomfort in what someone says, but we aren't sure we can see the truth in it. Even in these cases I have found it's best to reply with something like, "I recognize your point of view. I think I need to take some time to think about what you have said." There's nothing wrong with needing time to think and allowing yourself space to process the information that you've been presented. This way, you can come back to the conversation with clear eyes and all your faculties intact.

Learning to find and accept what is true can be one of the most difficult lessons to learn. When you make a conscious decision to find and acknowledge the truth instead of denying it, it can be hard to do so, or it can even feel awkward at first. Some of you will be undoing years of automatic programming in the process. The good news is that every time you choose to reverse your default way of reacting it gets easier. You'll notice how dropping your defense to the truth changes the course of your conversations for the better.

So how do we learn to fully accept what's true? By being honest with others and ourselves about our actions, without judging or evaluating them. By owning and taking responsibility for the words we use, our reactions, and our demeanor in the moment. At the same time, we all make mistakes, so when we realize when and where we've overreacted, been defensive, etc., we also know full well that these lapses are not a direct reflection of who we are all the time. We want to own our behavior so that our words and our actions are congruent. By accepting the truth of our words and actions, we are well on our way to stop the neverending volley of lying, exaggerating, gossiping, judging, and using language that hurts instead of helps.

🌸 Cultivate Communication

In your journal write down some examples of previous conversations in which you had difficulty accepting what was true. Instead of getting upset with yourself, focus on understanding why you couldn't accept the truth. What do you think it was about the situation that made it difficult or impossible for you to say, "You're right, I . . ."?

Now ask yourself, If I had been able to accept what was true, what might that have looked like? Could that have changed the conversation?

For a long time I fought against what was true, denying that my actions or reactions in a moment were a part of me. I disapproved and rejected these expressions because I saw them as confirmation that I was bad, wrong, or lesser than. But this bears repeating: just because you did something in that moment does not mean that action represents who you are all the time. When I was able to accept what was true, I was finally able to accept all the parts of who I am, knowing that the point was not to judge myself, but to understand why I said or did what I did to begin with.

As you practice this third step in learning how to listen to others, it will get easier. Next up is the final step: asking yourself if there is a way you can help.

Ask Yourself if There Is a Way You Can Help

I'll be the first to raise my hand and admit to making other people's lives harder than they needed to be. Someone would be talking about themselves and their needs, and I'd interrupt and make the conversation about me. I'd not listen, inevitably misinterpret what was being said, and if I didn't like what I heard I would assume the other person was judging, criticizing, or attacking me somehow. I never took the other person's perspective into consideration, focusing only on my own desires, fears, and insecurities. I equated the recognition of other people's goodness and positive qualities with my own lack of these things.

Can you see a pattern in this story? It all focuses on me. I was so in my own head, stuck in my soundtrack, that there was no way I could be helpful to whomever I was with because I wasn't really listening.

Once I realized that conversations were not a platform to puff myself up or to punish others for my insecurities, I let go of a lot of baggage and started listening. As a result of changing my communication habits and bringing the spirit of the bodhisattva into the way I converse with others, I've found that I can be helpful by paying attention to others' feelings, not encouraging destructive behavior, and last but certainly not least, simply being there.

How Can I Be Helpful to Others?

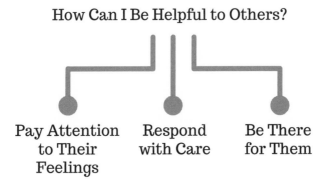

Pay Attention to Their Feelings

Respond with Care

Be There for Them

Pay Attention to Others' Feelings

If you remember from the first section, you learned how to look past your story and pay attention to your feelings. You also saw how helpful doing this could be, as releasing your feelings to the light of day is the first step toward healing. The same is true when it comes to listening to others, because if you can help them identify how they are feeling, you have begun the healing process for them as well.

Sometimes this isn't that hard. Like when you pick up the phone and it's your sister on the other line and you can immediately feel her tension and stress. You know her well, so you can tell something is wrong. For example, I met a friend for coffee and the minute she sat down I could sense something was off. I asked, "How are things?" That one question sent her into a tirade of expletives about what's not been going well for her at work, how there's too much pressure to churn out content in an inadequate amount of time, and she was ready to quit her job of ten years. That was the story.

"How are you feeling right now?" I asked. There was a pause in the conversation. I could sense she was searching. "Tired, exhausted, and overwhelmed," she said with a sigh. I could feel her release just by naming how she felt.

Prior to examining my communication method, I would have jumped into the story with her and probably said something like, "Those jackasses! Don't they see how hard you work? I never liked that boss of yours to begin with anyway. You are so right to be mad!" It's easy to want to corroborate with others to create kinship and a sense of belonging (much like we do when gossiping), but if all we do is keep one another focused on stories of hurt, then we aren't really being helpful. By inviting others to shift from the story to expressing how they feel, we are helping them move closer to healing what's happening inside.

One caveat: while it's good to help people identify their emotions if they are having trouble doing so themselves, be careful not to get stuck in their emotions. Your role as a good listener diminishes when you do so, because it's very difficult to remain balanced and ultimately helpful.

. . . .

❀ Cultivate Communication

The next time you're with someone who's upset, notice if he or she is identifying feelings or focusing exclusively on a story. If it's the latter, ask how he or she is feeling at that moment. Notice what happens if the person is able to articulate this.

Respond with Care

The next piece of being helpful to someone in communication is choosing how you respond when he or she looks to you for feedback. Using the example from the previous section, let's say that when my friend shared with me the difficulty she was having at her work, I replied by saying, "To heck with them! You should totally quit!"

As you can imagine, encouraging this action and in this way would not have been helpful. That's the other reason why it's important to not be drawn into the drama of the other person's story, as when you get caught up in the story you are more likely to suggest an unconscious reaction instead of a conscious response.

Because our goal is to help others suffer less, we want to take care when we respond, offering words that cultivate right action instead of encouraging behavior that produces more pain.

Buddhism teaches that all of us already have everything we need inside of us, but in my view sometimes we need another person to help us find our own answers. That's why having healthy communication habits is so beneficial.

Cultivate Communication

When someone asks you for feedback, a good rule of thumb is to "share your experience" rather than give advice. Rather than encouraging a friend to quit her job, I would say, "I know what it's like to feel overwhelmed at work. I've been there many times before. Is it possible you could speak with your boss and explain to him how you're feeling?"

By approaching your response from your experience, you are more likely to be helpful.

Here are some questions to consider when you're giving feedback on an issue:

- Can you think of a time you gave advice to someone that you weren't really qualified to give? What was the outcome?

- Can you think of a time someone shared his or her experience with you rather than giving you advice? How did this make you feel?

Be There for Them

By far the most important thing you can do to be helpful to someone is to simply be there for him or her. Mindfully listening, present in the moment, attentive to what the other person's heart wants to share with you.

Being there for others means letting them be who they are—not passing judgment, coming in with an agenda, or exaggerating or diminishing how they feel. Being there means listening as they express the wonderful moments of their lives, as well as their sorrowful ones. Being there means caring about others and wanting the best for them. Sometimes the hardest thing to do when we're listening to others is to let them be who they are. We have so much we want to say, or we may want to "fix" people, but most of the time we don't need to do anything more than just be there. Present, mindful, and listening. This is the most effective thing you can do to help. Being there for someone doesn't always involve using words; in fact, it is a form of communication that is beyond words. To be there is to accept the other person in all their joy and pain. Through the act of really listening, you are sending the message of "I'm here for you. You are not alone."

Here are three practical ways to show your support for someone in a conversation:

- Let the other person speak without any interruptions. (The average person listens for only seventeen seconds before interrupting.)
- Make eye contact.
- Give feedback or share experience only if it's requested.

❀ Cultivate Communication

Think about previous conversations in which you witnessed someone's joy or suffering. Were you able to be there for that person? To listen and to share in the joy or the sorrow? To be there to listen without judgment or an agenda? To let the person be who he or she really is?

Here are some additional tools to help you listen to the one you are with.

Make Eye Contact

When talking to your friends, or even the guy at the grocery store, make eye contact. Eye contact can help keep you in the present moment, focused on the other person, and it lets others know you are there for them.

Put Your Phone Down

In conversation, make sure you aren't scrolling through your phone. If you have developed a habit of constantly checking your phone, try making a commitment that you'll only look at your phone at certain times of day—for example, at nine in the morning and four in the afternoon.

Hold Your Tongue

Let others finish what they are saying before you start to speak.

Ask Questions

When you're in a conversation, take a step back periodically and ask yourself, What does this person need? How can I help this person suffer less? How can I be there for him or her?

Notice Yourself

When you're in a conversation, take a step back periodically and ask yourself, Am I judging the person I'm with? Do I think I know what they will say next? Am I getting lost in thought? If so, simply acknowledge this, gently let it go, and come back to the present moment.

Tell the Truth

If you know you aren't going to be able to give someone your full attention, let him or her know that this isn't a great time to talk and ask if you can reschedule. You want to be able to give your complete, undivided attention.

Use Encouraging Words

You can be agreeable without having to agree with everything a person says. Next time someone's sharing an opinion with you, try using one of the following phrases to show you understand:

- "I can see what you're saying."
- "What you said makes sense to me because . . ."
- "Although I may not agree, I get what you're saying."

Use Empathetic Words

It's important that people feel you're empathizing with them—otherwise, they may feel misunderstood, rejected, or ignored. Try using these phrases to show you're taking what they're saying to heart:

- "I can imagine you must feel/might have felt . . ."

- "I can see you're feeling . . ."

We've covered a lot of ground so far. What I'm hoping is that at this point you can see how important listening to yourself and others is in changing your communication style. Only after you know how to listen to yourself and to others in a kind, honest, nonjudgmental, and helpful way can you begin to speak in a way that others can hear, which means you're ready to move into the next phase: mindful speech.

In the next section we'll learn that while a Buddhist realizes that she is only responsible for what she says (not what others hear), she still takes great care to choose her words skillfully, so that the recipient is more likely to hear and understand them.

What to Remember

- How to listen to others: be present, see things from his or her perspective, accept what's true, and see if there is a way you can be helpful to this person.
- To be present: declutter your headspace. Notice the moment you're in.
- To be present in a conversation: focus your

attention, limit distractions, note distractions without judgment, and refocus your attention.

- To see things from another person's perspective: shift from I to we, think of the other person's unique experiences, and ask how you can see this situation differently.

- To accept what's true: be honest with others and yourself about your actions, without judging or evaluating them. Take responsibility for the words you use, your reactions, and your demeanor in the moment.

- To be helpful to others: pay attention to their feelings, respond with care, and be there for them. Remember: it's not your role to fix them; simply hold space for them.

Mindful Speech

Once we have perfected the art of listening to ourselves and others, we are now ready to try speaking mindfully. Mindful speech is the practice of bringing our attention to our words without judgment. It means we are aware of what we're saying and how we're saying it. We choose our words skillfully and speak consciously, concisely, and clearly so that the recipient is more likely to hear and understand us. In Buddhism, silence is considered a part of speech as well, which means we'll also pay attention to how we're using silence in conversation.

Speak Consciously, Concisely, and Clearly

All activities should be done with the intention of speaking so that another person can hear you, rather than using words that cause the barriers to go up and the ears to close.

—Pema Chödrön

When it comes to communication, speech is the number one tool we use to express ourselves. With our words comes great responsibility. We can use them in an attempt to create harmony, or we can use them to try to create suffering. When we use words without thinking, we can easily fall into the habit of lying, exaggerating, gossiping, and using language that isn't helpful. But when we take ownership of our speech we see the great responsibility we carry; we understand that how we speak to others and ourselves has the potential to lessen the suffering of others as well as change our lives and the lives of those we interact with for the better.

Because the words we choose are our responsibility, our goal on the bodhisattva path is to find ones that create a feeling of calm and foster a sense of goodwill. Furthermore, we take great care in expressing these words in a way that others can hear and understand. This includes choosing and speaking our words in such a way that others don't feel criticized, judged, or attacked. What I've found is that this can all be accomplished if we learn to speak using the three Cs: consciously, concisely, and clearly.

By being aware of the words we choose, using only the words we need, and expressing ourselves with clarity, we will vastly improve our communication, and this applies to everything—from our day-to-day interactions to those sensitive, tenuous conversations.

How to Speak to Others

Consciously

Concisely

Clearly

Speak Consciously

We've all been in situations in which we've said something we later regretted. Whether it was during an argument, in response to criticism, or even a joke that went too far, not only do we feel bad for what we said, but we also see the hurt we've caused someone. It's in the aftermath of these situations that we see how powerful our words can be.

If we start to pay conscious attention to our word choice before we speak, then we can choose wisely before it's too late. Every moment presents an opportunity to consciously choose how we express ourselves. We can choose to use words that encourage a sense of openness, understanding, and peace, or words that create stress, make others feel unappreciated, and provoke anxiety.

The first step to conscious speech involves slowing the conversation down.

Slow Down

The other day I slept over at my sister's place. In the morning she walked in and asked, "How did you sleep?" Without thinking I said, "Well, it was hot in here, but after some tossing and turning I was fine."

"I'm so sorry," she said.

"Oh, no. It's fine, really. I slept fine," I said again.

I didn't want to create a situation that made my sister feel bad, but because I didn't take it slow and actually think about what I was saying, my words affected her. This could have been avoided if I had thought before I spoke.

✿ Cultivate Communication

Think about a situation that you've been in when you said something without thinking. What effect did that have on the listener?

Now, if you had given yourself some time to think before you either responded or began the conversation, what could you have said differently?

When I talk with clients about slowing down, they often say, "Are you asking me to stop myself before I say something?" And the answer is yes. Why? Because a lot of what comes out of our mouths isn't helpful, necessary, or kind. When we slow down, we give ourselves the time to assess whether what we're about to say would enhance or improve the situation. If the answer is no, then we should likely choose to say nothing. If the answer is yes, then the pause gives us a chance to think of the best way to express ourselves. This may sound like a lot to do before you speak, but the more you practice the more natural it becomes. Soon, it becomes second nature to take your time before you express yourself so that you avoid blurting out something that you'll regret and that serves no helpful purpose.

Discerning what is worth a response and what is worthy of a simple acknowledgment instead means we have to change the rhythm of the conversation. We can slow the beats of the conversation down by drawing out the space between our thoughts and our words. Doing so helps us choose our words consciously. I like to think of it like this: we pause, take a breath, and then ask ourselves these important questions: Is it true? Is it kind? Is it helpful? The process would look something like the following:

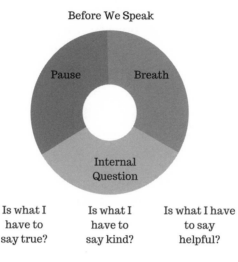

Before We Speak

Pause

Breath

Internal Question

| Is what I have to say true? | Is what I have to say kind? | Is what I have to say helpful? |

· ·

🌸 Cultivate Communication

Try using the pause, breathe, and question process before you say something. Remember, the point here is to slow down before you speak. Notice if doing so makes a difference in your communication with others.

Let's look at another example of how this might work in real life. Let's say you're in the grocery store and ready to check out. The woman ringing you up asks, "Did you find everything okay?" You're about to say, "Well, you didn't have any of the hummus I like, so I had to get another brand, but we'll see. Maybe I'll like it." Then you take a beat, a breath, and ask yourself, *Is my response true? Kind?*

Helpful? And while it may be true, you realize that there is nothing you can say that will help or improve the situation by expressing this. So instead you say, "I did, thanks."

If we slow down the process of interacting by using a pause, a breath, a question, and then we choose to speak, we give ourselves the time needed to choose our words wisely. Remember, it's easiest to begin practicing these steps in little interactions like the examples above. Once you have developed your new communication skills into a habit, you are much more likely to utilize them in more sensitive or potentially stressful situations.

Slowing down is only one way we help ourselves become and stay conscious when we're speaking with others. The next technique to help you do so is learning what is and isn't your responsibility within a conversation.

Know What You Are Responsible For

Remember that a bodhisattva is someone who hears the cries of the world and endeavors to limit suffering. For the purposes of communication, a bodhisattva would choose her words carefully so that her listener may understand and be helped by them.

That being said, it's important to remember that while you do your best in being conscious of which words you choose and how you use them, you are ultimately not responsible for someone else's reaction to them. Your speech is what you control, but you can't control how those words are interpreted.

Now here's the rub. The reverse is also true. People don't have the power to "set you off" with their words unless you give them that power. If someone says something you don't like, or even hurls an insult your way, and you react emotionally (internally or externally), the reaction is yours, and you're the only one responsible for it. Not reacting to someone else's words is one of the hardest things to master, and very few people, if any, do so perfectly all the time. An in-depth discussion of this is beyond the scope of this book, but I would be remiss not to mention it here. For our purposes, the point is to become aware of what you can and cannot control when communicating.

There are three pieces to any conversation: the speaker, the listener, and the conversation itself. What the speaker and listener have in common is the conversation. When you are the speaker, you are responsible for your words, your actions, your reactions. When you are the listener, you are responsible for the same things. The balance here can be difficult, especially when it's necessary to say something that another person likely won't like or won't want to hear.

For example, after having a difficult conversation with a friend awhile back, I explained that I needed to take a day to think about what she had said, and I asked if we could speak about it again the following day. She agreed, but when we met up the next day I could tell she was even more upset than the previous day. She began our conversation by saying something like, "I think you were so selfish yesterday. You told me you needed to take some time to think things over and get back to me. Well, that ruined the rest of my day, because I was so worried and upset about things that I couldn't concentrate."

I didn't like that my friend felt hurt by my words, but I also knew that her response to my words wasn't my responsibility. I was responsible for my words and the conversation, and by taking time for me to collect my thoughts, I knew I could come back to the conversation with a clear head and be able to express myself in a way that was honest, kind, and helpful. If I didn't allow myself that time, the conversation wouldn't have served either of us. My intention was for the greater good; to create a scenario in which we could have a conversation that was honest and kind while at the same time discussing some difficult issues.

"I hear that you are upset," I replied, "and I wish that weren't the case. Please know that my intention in asking for a break yesterday was not to upset you further, but was rather to allow myself time to think about the important issues you raised yesterday. I care about you and only want what's best. Do you think we can talk about those things now and try to find a solution?"

Once I acknowledged that my friend was upset and explained my position again, she was ready to continue the conversation from the previous day. Notice how I did not respond by pointing out that: 1) she agreed to delay, and 2) her allowing the postponement to "ruin her day" was her choice and had nothing to do with me. A reply like that was not necessary, nor would it have been useful or kind. Instead, it would have likely prompted more ill feelings in my friend, preventing the opportunity for the healthy communication that ultimately took place.

"Fixing" Others

There was a time in my life when I thought it was my responsibility to "fix" the other people in my life, helping them to get out of any funk they were in. The more I assumed the role of "fixer," the more some people in my life would look to me to do so. I played this role so well that I would even stand around as some people took out their frustration for whatever was happening in their own lives on me. As you can imagine, this was not creating fertile ground for healthy conversations to take place.

What I have learned is that if someone is having a bad day or a difficult time, there is nothing wrong with trying to make the person feel better, as long as you remember that ultimately it's up to him or her to have the self-awareness to see what the trouble is and then decide what needs to happen in order to feel better. It's the other person's responsibility to learn how to alleviate his or her own pain. We can acknowledge the pain, be there for the pain, listen to the pain, but it's not our pain to resolve, nor is it within our power to do so.

When we understand what we are and are not responsible for in a conversation, we can consciously choose words that help us avoid conflict and promote a healthy dialogue. For example, below are some interactions and possible ways the conversations can go, where each person knows what he or she is and is not responsible for.

After getting off the phone with her boyfriend, Sally goes out and meets her friends. "What's wrong?" they ask. "Jake lost his job. And he was so upset on the phone that he started getting angry at me for nothing," Sally replies. "So what happened?" they asked.

Unhealthy dialogue: Sally says, "I kept trying to make him feel better, but he just wouldn't listen. Finally he got so mad at me he slammed the phone down. I'm so hurt and upset."

Healthy dialogue: Sally says, "I let him know that I was there for him if he needed me, but because I knew nothing good was going to come from continuing the conversation right then, I let him know I had to go."

You've been working really hard on your pitch for a client. After your presentation they say, "It's not what we're looking for. We were hoping you would be able to really show us something that would set us apart from our competitors."

Unhealthy dialogue: You reply, "Well, if you would've given me more direction I would have been able to give you what you were looking for. I'm good at what I do, but I'm not a mind reader. "

Healthy dialogue: You reply, "Can you tell me a little more about your vision? I want to understand better where you are coming from so I can create something unique that will help your company achieve its goals."

It's opening night and you're excited. You call your mom and right away she asks, "So are you ready?"

Unhealthy dialogue: "Why wouldn't I be ready?" you answer. "It's opening night." Your mom says, "Oh good. I just remember that one time when you forgot your lines." You reply, "Why did you bring that up? Now I am going to worry about it all night!"

Healthy dialogue: You reply, "Yes, I am ready!" Your mom says, "Oh good. I just remember that one time when you forgot your lines." You say, "I do too—that's why I am better prepared this time."

🌼 Cultivate Communication

Before you go into your next meeting or an important conversation, answer the following questions:

- What's your intention or goal for the conversation?
- What points do you want to get across?
- What do you want to know or learn from the other person/people?

By writing down your goals, what you hope to communicate, and what you want to know or learn, you can more easily stay focused on having a healthy, productive dialogue. Knowing how to edit out the unnecessary distractions from our speech keeps sentences honest, to the point, and free of judgment, which makes it easier for others to hear and understand us.

Knowing what we are responsible for within a conversation helps prevent us from falling back into old communication patterns that promote suffering. Here's a graph to help you remember what you are responsible for within a conversation:

Our Responsibility in a Conversation

SPEAKER		LISTENER
Your words		Your words
Your actions		Your actions
Your reactions	Health of conversation	Your reactions
Your thoughts		Your thoughts
Your feelings		Your feelings
Your silence		Your silence

Without slowing down or knowing what is and is not our responsibility, it's difficult to choose our words consciously in a conversation. When we don't speak consciously, we are more likely to fall into automatic reactions that go against the elements of right speech.

· ·

🌸 Cultivate Communication

In the coming days, notice in conversations when you hear others attempt to shift responsibility for their reactions onto someone else. If you watch television or the movies, notice when the characters on screen do it as well. The point here isn't to judge the behavior or point it out to anyone. Just begin a practice of noticing when this occurs in others, as that will make it easier to notice it in yourself.

Speak Concisely

If you've ever talked to a novelist or screenplay writer, you may have heard about the idea of putting limits on a story. The more limits the writer uses, the easier it is not only for the writer to tell the story, but also for the audience to understand it. The same rings true in day-to-day conversation. We get the sense in our world that more is better, but when it comes to communication, the more we pare down our words, the more expressive we can actually be.

Another practical benefit of speaking concisely is related to the previous section, as the fewer words we use, the more likely we are to choose them consciously. This makes it much easier to avoid lying, exaggerating, gossiping, or saying something that isn't helpful.

It's interesting how applying the elements of right speech can naturally help keep our speech concise. Look at some of the examples that follow, and notice that when the answer conforms to the elements of right speech it also corresponds to using words concisely.

Question	Not Using the Elements of Right Speech	Using Right Speech
Next time could you make sure to empty the teakettle after you make tea?	I leave the water in there because I'm going to be using it again. It's just water, what's the problem?	Yes.
Do you want to grab dinner tonight?	I can't because I have to go pick up a friend from the airport. She's having some issues with her husband so I said I'd help her out.	Tonight I can't, but later this week would be great.
I have tickets for a concert next weekend. Do you want to go?	I thought you didn't like live music. I'm the one who loves concerts.	That would be great—thanks!
I need to stop eating so much.	Me too. I feel like I've gained so much weight in the last week.	(You say nothing.)

Filtering our words through the four elements of right speech makes it easier for us to rein them in.

So this sounds great in theory, but in practice how do you put the kibosh on your extras, especially when addressing difficult topics? By learning to cut the fat from the conversation.

Cut the Fat

I mentioned a moment ago that limiting our words can actually make us more expressive. That's because when we use fewer words, we can be conscious to choose the ones that most accurately describe how we feel, and using fewer words can make it easier for our listener to understand and respond to us.

Take a look at the following sentences and see if you can spot any ways that cutting them down might enhance the conversation.

- We're not bringing the kids to the wedding because it's just too much of a hassle.
- Could this woman make up her mind already? I really want to order.
- This needs to be turned in by the end of the day or else you're going to hear it from the boss.

Here are the same bits of conversation with brackets around the parts that are not improving the interaction.

- We're not bringing the kids to the wedding [because it's just too much of a hassle].
- [Could this woman make up her mind already?] I really want to order.
- This needs to be turned in by the end of the day [or else you're going to hear it from the boss].

Besides cutting all that isn't in line with the rules of right speech, what's also being cut are the parts that could distract your listener, making it difficult for him or her to understand what you're trying to get across. So by speaking concisely, we help others and ourselves stay focused on what's important.

❀ Cultivate Communication

Think about a past situation when you maybe said too much and the result was that your listener either had trouble following you or perhaps was hurt or offended by your words. Now think about if you had applied the elements of right speech to this situation. What parts of the conversation would have changed?

Speak Clearly

There's a Pickles cartoon by Brian Crane that shows Opal asking her husband, Earl, to unplug the kitchen sink. Earl says he'll take care of it ASAP. Opal says, "Great!" Then when their grandson asks what "ASAP" means, Earl says, "After September, August, Possibly."

While the definition of ASAP is widely known, it's still a pretty vague term. "As soon as possible" to you may mean when you have the time; to someone else, it may mean right away, before doing anything else.

Vague language creates ambiguity in conversations, which if it isn't addressed can lead to difficulties later that could have been avoided with a little planning and fore-thought. How, then, do we express a need clearly so that the listener can understand us? By saying what we mean, asking for what we need, and being specific.

Saying What We Mean, Asking for What We Need, and Being Specific

Bryan and I were in an airport restaurant waiting for our flight to Vegas when he told me he wanted to watch the hockey game the next morning. "The game starts at eleven. They're in the finals. It's a big one." I felt my insides swell and start firing. Bryan could sense my reaction and asked, "Are you upset?" In the past, I would have said *no*, which would have been a lie, and I would have gotten even angrier that he couldn't read my mind and understand why I was mad at him.

But now, having worked on my communication issues, I paused and said, "Yes. I'm a little upset because this is our getaway trip to Vegas, and I wish you would be spending all the time there with me instead of watching the hockey game. I know neither of us thought your favorite team would be in the finals when we booked this weekend months ago, though, and I understand—and I hope they win!" I smiled, he smiled, and just like that, the uneasy feeling was gone.

In this situation I explained exactly how I felt and why I felt that way, when in times past I would have lied and told myself a story about how he should have known how I really felt, and then gotten angrier when he didn't.

Bryan, on the other hand, put into place the next tool for achieving clarity in speech: he asked for the information he needed. Specifically, Bryan asked if I was upset that he would be watching the game, and this set the stage for continued open conversation. Imagine if it had gone the other way, if Bryan had instead sensed that I was upset and rather than asking for clarification got upset and told himself a story like, *I can't believe she is so upset that I want to watch my favorite team*, which in reality wasn't true. I was a little annoyed that we would miss a couple of hours together on our vacation, but it wasn't that big of a deal. Had he not asked, he could have assumed the worst and exaggerated the situation in his mind.

Instead, he took care of his need, to ask, and I took care of my need, to answer. As a result, we were both able to express ourselves honestly in a situation that could have easily turned into something much bigger if we hadn't been clear in our speech.

Asking for what we need is a crucial tool to bring clarity to our communications and ultimately changes in our relationships. I have been in many sessions with clients who have told me about the behavior of a coworker, spouse, or friend that is causing them suffering only to find out that they have never expressed their hurt or irritation, instead assuming that the other person should know, or feeling that it was somehow inappropriate to ask for what was needed. But if we don't include the critical element of asking for what we need, we do ourselves and the other person a disservice. We may make a thousand assumptions instead, all of which could be wrong.

After we ask for what we need, it's then up to the other person to answer our question, commit to our request, or do neither. If he or she makes a change, great! If not, then it's up to us to decide whether this behavior is something we can accept in our lives, or if another change is necessary.

Here are some other common scenarios when asking for what you need can make all the difference:

- You're frustrated because your significant other has been really busy lately and hasn't made time for you. You might say, "When you cancel our dates at the last minute I feel frustrated.

I know you aren't trying to upset me; however, next time could you please let me know the day before if you can't make it?"

- You're feeling anxious at work because a coworker is moving ahead on a project and you're not sure about some details that you're responsible for. You might say, "When you don't cc me on e-mails I feel out of the loop, and I want to make sure I don't miss anything. Could you please make sure to cc me when you're sending a group exchange in the future?"

- The neighbor lets her dog out at 5:30 every morning, and he barks nonstop, waking you up. One afternoon, you knock on her door and say, "I don't know if you are aware of this, but your dog wakes me up every morning when he comes outside. Would it be possible for you to keep him inside until 7 a.m.?"

To express our needs clearly the ask is key. But we also want to make sure that we're being specific.

Be Specific

I began this section with the anecdote about a cartoon, and the differing meanings of ASAP. (I have a friend who says he understands ASAP to mean he will do it "sometime before he dies.") By being specific in our communications, whether we are asking or answering, we reduce the chances of a misunderstanding.

Take for example the barking dog scenario. What if you went to the neighbor and just said, "Can you let your dog out later in the morning?" She may agree and be thinking that 6:15 is "later in the morning." And she would be right. But you were thinking 7 a.m. So by being specific in what you mean, you head off a future issue.

Examples like these are the easiest to spot and implement, and doing so can make a world of difference in your communication. Let's look at a few more examples that are a little more subtle.

I have an old friend that I run into every six months or so, and the exchange is always the same. We spend a few minutes catching up, embrace, and say good-bye with something like, "This was great. We really need to catch up more often." Finally, the last time it happened, I said, "Let's make it a point to talk by phone or meet for coffee once a month." She agreed, and by being specific and making a commitment together, our relationship has grown as a result.

Another vague phrase I would catch myself saying all the time is, "Do you want to . . . ?" instead of "Can you . . . ?" For instance, I would say to Bryan, "Do you want to help me fold the laundry?" instead of "Can you help me fold the laundry?" The latter is being specific with what I really wanted, while the former was an entirely different question.

. . . .

✤ Cultivate Communication

Let's practice bringing these three teaching points together. Can you think of a current issue that you need to speak with someone about? This can be something large or small. On a piece of paper, write out what you want to communicate to that person. As you write, be sure to 1) say exactly what you mean, 2) ask for what you need, and 3) be specific. By limiting your writing to these three components, you can leave off any extraneous words that may cloud the issue or provoke a defensive reaction in the other person.

For example, I have a friend who drives his teenage daughter to school in the morning, and because she often wasn't ready to go when he wanted to, he was late for work. He wrote down what he needed to communicate to her, and it went something like this: "When you aren't ready to leave for school in the morning I feel frustrated because then I'm late for work. Could you be ready at 7:30 so we can leave by 7:45? That way I'll get to work on time."

What to Remember

The three Cs of communicating: Speak consciously, concisely, and clearly.

- To speak consciously: slow the conversation down (beat, breathe, question) and know what you are and aren't responsible for in the conversation. (You're responsible for your words, actions, and reactions. You are not responsible for the other person's words, reactions, and actions.)
- To speak concisely: cut the fat by eliminating anything that doesn't qualify as right speech and enhance the conversation. Express yourself with the purpose and point in mind.
- To speak clearly: say what you mean, incorporate the ask into your conversations, and be specific.

✿ Cultivate Communication

Repeat this affirmation each morning for a week:
"Today I am going to speak consciously, concisely, and clearly."

To really master expressing ourselves requires that we are conscious, concise, and clear. Implementing the three Cs changes our communication routine by taking the guessing and assuming out of our conversations. While we've focused here on enhancing our conversations using our words, we'll next get into how we can use silence as a way to improve our interactions.

Use the Language of Silence

Saying nothing . . . sometimes says the most.

—Emily Dickinson

As a young teenager, I remember riding in the car once on my way home from ballet class and mouthing off to my mom for being five minutes late picking me up. "What was that?" she asked. I sat silently and looked out the window. "Excuse me," she said again. I didn't respond, instead crossing my arms and fuming.

This isn't the type of silence I'm going to advocate in this chapter.

All joking aside, silence still plays a pivotal role in how I communicate with others, but now it's in a much more helpful fashion. In years past I mostly used silence to exaggerate my displeasure with a situation. It was only after I was introduced to mindful communication that I saw how helpful silence could actually be in conversations. The more I monitored my silence, the more I saw it for what it is, a language in itself. In this section we'll look at how you can use the language of silence to enhance your conversations as opposed to stifling them.

Specifically, silence can be used to express compassion and intimacy, to balance interaction, and to be helpful. In doing so, silence can actually become a part of right speech instead of a tool for its opposite.

Silence as Compassion and Intimacy

When I was younger there was a phrase I'd hear a lot, "the silent treatment." "Oh, she's giving him the silent treatment," someone would say, and the crux of the situation was that she was mad or otherwise upset, and that somehow the "silent treatment" was an effective means of getting her feelings of anger or hurt across to her partner.

That was my understanding of an effective communication technique when I was in grade school. You'd think the silent treatment would have disappeared along with the other misunderstandings of youth, but it simply changed names. Today, we refer to the silent treatment as one aspect of passive-aggressive behavior, or when we use the language of silence as a tool to hurt, blame, and punish others. Remember this graphic from earlier?

I pretend it's fine that my partner is going out with his friends instead of coming to family dinner. (I'm lying.)

My partner thinks I'm telling the truth, so he goes out with his friends.

I'm angry that he went out with his friends, so when he gets home I'm passive-aggressive, saying that I'm fine. Really. Nothing's wrong. (Again, I'm lying.)

Both people suffer. I suffer because I'm not getting what I want. He suffers because I'm now being mean to him.

Our first step is to pay attention to how we use silence in our conversations, especially in stressful or uncomfortable situations. If we notice how we use silence in a hurtful way, the easier it is for us to change our behavior. Instead of falling into the old pattern, we can come into the present moment and identify the feelings behind our silence. We may choose to share our feelings at that moment, or we may choose to wait first and try to see the situation from the other person's perspective, and then ask how he or she is feeling. In either case, we are using silence as a means of deepening the conversation instead of keeping it stuck in the shallow waters of scorn. We begin to see silence in the conversation as an opportunity to see the other person with friendly eyes, to see those gaps in speech as an opportunity to experience love and kindness, rather than silently wishing pain and suffering upon someone. By seeing the other through loving eyes, we change our silence from a tool of anger into a vehicle for compassion. Using silence in this way takes conscious effort at first, but once you start it gets easier, and you can develop a new habit that equates silence with an opportunity to be compassionate.

Silence as Balance

I first noticed that silence could be used to promote balance in conversations when I was with my friend in Valencia, Spain. We were lying on the beach, the sun shining bright, the mist from the waves chilling the air every now and again. Both of us were reading. My friend then rolled over and said, "This book is really interesting." I waited for her to continue but she paused.

I put my book down and sat up, preparing to listen more intently. She started talking, but she paused after major points, which helped me to focus, listen, and process what she was saying. I also noticed that by pausing she was better able to choose the right words to express what she wanted to convey. By creating gaps in her speech, she made it easier for me to listen, and in truth it was the silence that actually caught my attention.

When she'd finished, she asked what I thought about what she had just explained. This simple process of pausing had drawn me in, and had better transitioned the dialogue from what she thought and opened it up to what I thought. I marveled at how even and balanced the conversation felt.

From then on, I was hooked on using what I call gaps in conversation as a way to transition away from I into We, reminding myself that there are two people; this is a conversation, not a one-way street. Using gaps can help us keep our focus on the purpose of communicating. Gaps are a clear recognition of the other's presence within a conversation, and a way into shared dialogue.

● ●

🌸 Cultivate Communication

In the next conversation you have, try to use pauses to create gaps in your speech. See if you can ask the person you're with "What do you think?" or "What are your thoughts?" Note how the conversation opens into a shared experience. Both of you are in it together instead of one person being in it for him- or herself.

Like the spoken word, silence is a language that can be used for good or bad. Because we want to lessen the suffering of others and ourselves, our goal is to use silence to enhance our communication rather than using it as a barrier to communication.

Silence as a Way to Help

While both of the previous examples could be identified as ways to use silence to be helpful, another way we can view the language of silence as helpful is that being silent gives us the time we need to tap into the present moment and simply be. This silence is an opportunity to drop whatever stories are currently running in our minds and pay attention to what's happening right in front of us.

Buddhist nun Pema Chödrön teaches a form of pausing

practice that accomplishes this quite nicely. In her version, someone rings a bell every now and then to interrupt conversations or whatever is going on. When the bell sounds, everyone stops what they are doing and pauses for the length of three breaths. Afterward, everything picks back up where it left off, but with the benefit of having taken a moment to ground in the present moment.

Sometimes it's easier to practice pausing when you're in a feel-good situation—maybe when you're snuggling with someone you love, or walking down the street looking up at the sky. These moments lend themselves to taking in our surroundings and being grateful and appreciative for what's in our lives. Pausing in the good moments brings us into the present—we become aware of our lives. And pausing in the more difficult moments gives us the opportunity to find the good within the moment; to connect to the other person again, and decide how best to express ourselves. In this way, silence can be a very helpful language.

✴ Cultivate Communication

Silence gets a bad rap in today's world, as it's all too common to refer to silence in conversations as "uncomfortable." But is that true? Must we always be talking?

In the course of the next few days, practice "purposeful silence" in your interactions with others. When you notice you are about to say something that is more of a gap-filler and designed to eliminate silence (the proverbial "How's the weather?" type of interaction), purposefully choose silence instead. This is often easiest to do at first with those you are closest to. If you like, share that you are consciously practicing using silence. Notice how the ability to be silent in the presence of others creates intimacy and a connection to the present moment.

What to Remember

Silence can be used to express compassion and intimacy, as a way to equalize an interaction, and as an opportunity to center us in the present moment.

- How to turn silence into compassion: notice silence—how you're using it, what the feeling is behind it—and see things from the other person's perspective with loving eyes.
- How to use silence as an equalizer: use gaps when speaking to include others in the conversation, turning the conversation away from I to we.
- How to use silence to enhance overall communication: take time to think about your interactions to make sure they are kind, honest, and helpful.

In the final section, we will visit the topic of silence again, mindfully. You might be thinking, wait—we just did a chapter on silence! But I promise this one is different. Here the focus is not on using silence as a part of speech, but on creating silence within so that we become honest, free of judgment and exaggeration, and helpful in our speech.

Mindful Silence

Mindful silence is sitting for five, ten, twenty minutes or more, in silence with a focused attention. Noticing our thoughts and feelings, but not attaching to them; simply accepting them and then letting them go to come back to the focus of our attention, which can be our breath, our body, a mantra, etc. Mindful silence in this context is meditation.

Although this is the last section in the practice of communicating like a Buddhist, it is the one that makes all the others easier to do. This could possibly be the most important section of the book, as without this last tool it would be almost impossible to use the elements of right speech in conversation. Why? Because the practice of meditation lets us be who we are as we are, without any shame or judgment attached. We sit with ourselves alone, bare, not to be judged, but to be accepted. It is only when we accept ourselves that we can do the same for others. Once we accept ourselves, we are better able to leave the lying, exaggerating, gossiping, and hurtful language behind. We become our own version of a bodhisattva.

Meditation

Who looks outside, dreams; who looks inside, awakens.

—Carl Jung

While learning the elements of right speech and figuring out how to apply them to my daily life, the one step that made them easiest to implement was the practice of meditation. I imagine many of you reading this are familiar with meditation already, but for those of you who are not, I will give a brief overview of meditation here before moving on to specific meditations designed to improve your communication skills.

Meditation is a difficult topic for many people. You might think of meditation as being a bit "out there," or as something reserved for spiritual straight-A students. Just mentioning the word provokes uneasiness in some. And it's understandable. In our modern lives we aren't really accustomed to stopping, to doing literally nothing for five or ten minutes. How are you supposed to just stop thinking? What if you feel like you don't have five minutes to relax? How will you find time to sit and breathe? Do you have to be a Buddhist or spiritual in order to meditate?

Well, first off, you don't have to be anything to meditate! And second, the goal, which you'll see later on, is not to stop yourself from thinking but simply to acknowledge that you are thinking. It is a practice of noticing without judgment, letting go, noticing without judgment, letting go. Perhaps you recognize the mantra of noticing and letting go from previous sections.

What Is Meditation?

Meditation is an ancient and modern practice that reduces stress and helps train the brain to be less reactive and more responsive. For me, meditation is a practice of observation without judgment. It is a practice of sitting, focusing, and refocusing. The focus can be your breath, sounds, or a phrase, but the point is that the practice of always coming back to your focus keeps you anchored in the present moment. Letting your thoughts go into the past and the future, noticing them, and then letting them go without any judgment and coming back to the present focus. This practice is very similar to teachings I have described regarding communication; we are constantly coming back to the conversation we're in, refocusing on the moment and the person or people we're with. Forever letting go of our thoughts, no matter the content, and coming back to the moment we're in and starting again. Remember this visual?

Process of Being Present in a Conversation

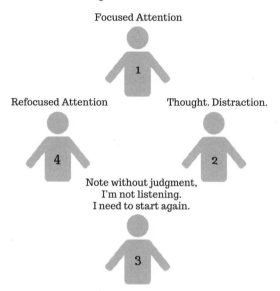

Focused Attention

1

Refocused Attention

Thought. Distraction.

4

2

Note without judgment,
I'm not listening.
I need to start again.

3

There are many different types of meditation (sitting, walking, lying down, etc.), but for our purposes let's begin by finding a place where you can be alone for a few moments without distraction.

Start by sitting on a cushion with your legs crossed and your knees below your hips, or sitting on a chair with your feet firmly planted on the ground, hands resting on your thighs. You want to sit up straight, assuming an upright posture, and your gaze should be about six inches in front of you. You could also close your eyes if you prefer. Although you're sitting tall, you don't want to force the position; it should be comfortable. Once you're in position, take a couple breaths to center into the present moment and focus your attention on your breath.

Bring your attention to the rise and fall of your chest as you breathe. Now rest your attention on the pauses between the breaths. When your mind starts wandering, simply note that you're thinking, and bring your attention back to your breath.

Many first-time meditations go something like this: You close your eyes and start thinking, *Okay, focus on my breath . . . inhale . . . exhale . . . I need to send that e-mail . . . inhale . . . exhale . . . I forgot to put food in the dog bowl—wait, did I put the food in the dog bowl? . . .*

As you focus on your breath, your mind may spin with minor explosions of thoughts about things, people, ideas, emotions, and feelings. All of this can leave you thinking, *Oh no, I'm doing this wrong,* but the truth is that this is what happens to the vast majority of us, and what you want to do is simply notice the thoughts and what's there, and then gently come back to your breath. The moment you notice you're following a story line, that's your cue to come back to your breath. What this teaches us is how to observe our thoughts without becoming consumed by or attached to them. Start slowly, doing this for five or ten minutes, and gradually work up to longer periods of time. It helps if you can find an instructor or group to meditate with, as there is something about doing this with others that makes it easier on all of us.

Think about how this practice can help you communicate with others and yourself. By practicing this acknowledging and letting go, you will be better able to detach from the stories you get stuck in and come back to the present moment. You will begin to witness other people's story lines and be able to detach from trying to fix or solve them. You'll see what doesn't help you to enhance the conversation and learn to let those things go. Meditation is how you learn to listen to yourself without judgment, to become aware of your words and your facial expressions, to be present for yourself and others. Along with being engaged with the present, practicing meditation can help you to move away from being reactive to situations, people, and things, and instead become more responsive.

Practicing Meditation

Meditation helps us accept what is happening in the moment. This allows us to be more open and compassionate with others, and to see situations and circumstances more clearly; but it is not a one-time-only kind of deal. Meditation is never accomplished, finished, or mastered. It is a practice that, when cultivated, reminds us that at any point in our communications we can refocus, come back to our breath, and start again.

For our purposes I want to focus on five kinds of meditation:

- Meditating to Enhance Self-Compassion
- Meditating to Implement Honesty
- Meditating to See Things from Another Person's Perspective
- Meditating to Detach from the Story Line
- Meditating to Balance or Rebalance Communication

Incorporating any one of these into your day will help you ditch the old communication routine for good. I'll give you an overview of each, and invite you to investigate them further on your own, making them a part of your ongoing practice.

Meditating to Enhance Self-Compassion

To speak kind, honest, and helpful words with others, we learned that we must first start with ourselves. With roots in Buddhism, this Loving Kindness Meditation is a technique used to foster compassion for the self and also for others. There are different forms of this meditation; however, the practice that follows uses phrases that you repeat silently first, to others, then toward yourself, and later to the world. From the following phrases choose two that speak to you:

> May you feel loved.
> May you feel peace.
> May you be free from suffering.
> May you feel safe.
> May you know joy.
> May you be happy.

With your eyes closed, bring to mind someone you love and cherish. See him or her in front of you. Let yourself feel what sensations or feelings arise when you see this person. Go ahead and hug this person and silently say your two phrases *(May you feel loved; May you know joy)*. Sit here for a minute, feeling what comes up for you.

Then shift your attention to yourself. Place your hand on your heart and repeat the two phrases to yourself *(May you feel loved; May you know joy)*. Sit in this feeling; let whatever is coming up for you be as it is.

Then shift your attention to someone you don't really know—your mailman, the barista at the coffee shop—and repeat the two phrases, again letting yourself sit with the emotion arising.

From there, picture all beings in the world and again repeat the two phrases. Finish the meditation by coming back to yourself repeating the two phrases again as a blessing *(May you feel love; May you know joy)*. Then take a couple of deep breaths and slowly open your eyes.

Practicing this type of meditation will help you see yourself as someone to be cared for and cherished, and as the lovable and genuinely good person you are.

Meditating to Implement Honesty

In the Buddhist tradition, *Vipassana* means "to see things as they really are." And if you think back to the first element of right speech, the goal is to start seeing the truth of situations instead of what we believe them to be or want them to be. This can be hard to do, but Vipassana meditation can help.

Vipassana meditation teaches us to observe ourselves without judgment, accepting who we are exactly as we are. By doing so, we are committing to sit with ourselves in our best and worst of times, and we begin to see our habits and actions clearly. We learn that if we want to see ourselves honestly, we can't ignore certain pieces and accept others—because then we aren't complete or whole. By becoming honest with ourselves we then become honest with others. We begin to see who we are through meditation and to accept what we find.

Before discovering Buddhism, I was often unable to admit the truth of a situation or take responsibility for myself and my actions. I defended myself, explained myself, made excuses, and was the queen of passive-aggressive behavior. As I started practicing Vipassana meditation, I learned little by little how to accept the truth of a situation and my responsibility within it. The more I practiced, the more honest I became with myself, and the more honest I was able to be with others.

Meditating to See Things from Another Person's Perspective

Tonglen, meaning "giving and taking," or "giving and receiving," is a meditation practice found in Tibetan Buddhism. Tonglen meditation helps bring in suffering and let out compassion. That may sound strange at first, as many people question why one would want to intentionally bring suffering into a meditation practice. But by inviting it in, we are accepting hurt and our pain as a part of us. We aren't trying to get over it or push it to the side; we're saying yes to it. By feeling our own suffering, we are better able to honor the suffering of others.

This meditation is extremely helpful for establishing a new communication style because it focuses on one of the most difficult pieces—putting ourselves in the other person's position. For us to keep a discussion kind, honest, and helpful we have to learn compassion. Without compassion there is no dialogue. Without compassion there is no shift in how we see a situation.

The first time I did this meditation, I was asked to envision someone I knew who was hurting, someone I wanted to help. On the inhale, I was asked to imagine myself in that person's situation, experiencing her fears. To see the world through her eyes. I was asked to think about what she most needed. I was asked to feel it fully, taking it in so she would be relieved. On the exhale, I was to imagine whatever would bring her calm.

Take a moment to think of someone you've had a difficult conversation with or someone who causes strong automatic reactions in you when you're in the same room. Close your eyes and see the person. Can you move into this person's world? See what situations may look like from his or her perspective? Can you begin to see why this person speaks in his or her particular way, or reacts in that way? What do those reactions yell out for? What feeling might this person be seeking? Open your eyes and write down what you felt and what you think this person needs. The next time you're with this person, look over this page before you meet.

If we meditate to experience compassion, the easier it is for us to be compassionate when the moment arises. When we find ourselves in a difficult communication situation, we can pause, breathe, and come to this place we've cultivated through meditation. And the more we practice, the easier it is to return to this place when it's needed.

Meditating to Detach from the Story Line

While the previous meditations are great to practice regularly, this detachment meditation is something I practice after a discussion in which I felt I reacted, spoke meanly, postured myself as better, or was on the receiving end of someone else's anger and pain. Some may do this meditation daily, but I save it for those moments when I really need to let go of overwhelming emotion; when I get absorbed;

when I really need to drop the obsession over the story to understand what the feeling underneath a reaction was. Let me explain how to do this meditation.

Assume your meditation position and close your eyes. Inhale and exhale to center yourself. Think of the stories you've been gathering. What have you been obsessing over or talking about with others again and again? See the story and invite the feeling behind it. Ask yourself, *What do I feel? What am I really feeling right now? How do I feel hurt?* Once you conjure these emotions, put your hand on your heart and say, "I see you." Say it as many times as you need to. "I see you. I know you're hurting. I'm here for you." Continue to comfort yourself in the meditation for several minutes.

When I've reacted to someone or said something that wasn't in line with the elements of right speech, instead of getting stuck in the shame cycle, making myself feel worse, I detach from my own judgment by asking for forgiveness and forgiving myself. I close my eyes and focus on what I've done to cause someone else harm. I see the pain I've caused and I say, "Please forgive me for my reaction. I see you're upset by my reaction. Please forgive me." Then I turn the words on myself. *I forgive you for your reaction. I forgive you for your reaction.*

When I first did this meditation, I cried. I'd never been kind to myself in situations when I was wrong before. I'd punish myself, thinking I needed to be scolded for bad behavior. But I now know that what I really needed was to notice and admit to the behavior, understand it didn't define who I was as bad, and view it as an opportunity to learn, care for myself, and start again.

Meditating to Balance or Rebalance Communication

According to yoga philosophy, chakras are energy centers in the body that when in line help us live honestly, creatively, equally, joyously, and energetically, and when out of line create deficiencies in the mind and body. There are seven major chakras in the body, but for our purposes we're going to focus on the vishuddha, or throat chakra, as that is the chakra associated with communication. Below I've outlined what a balanced versus imbalanced throat chakra looks like.

Chakra	In Balance	Out of Balance
vishuddha (throat)	You express yourself easily and clearly and say just what you want and need.	You pretend everything is fine when it isn't.
	You communicate mindfully, using the elements of right speech.	You don't believe what you feel is worthy of discussion.
		You are self-righteous and talkative or soft-spoken.

While we may identify right away with some of the characteristics of a balanced throat chakra, other times we can see what may be off by noticing what we're feeling physically. Following is a meditation to bring balance to your throat chakra.

Lie down on your back and close your eyes. As you inhale and exhale, imagine your breath moving through all parts of your body. Now put your attention on your throat. Does it feel dry? Tight? Clogged? Do you feel any aching or soreness? Imagine you are inhaling a white light into the throat area, and then exhale any feelings of discomfort or blackness. Inhale white light and exhale the clutter in the area. Do this meditation for several minutes, visualizing your throat clearing of anything that may be clogging it up.

Each chakra has a mantra associated with it. The mantra for the throat chakra is *hum*. According to the Hindu tradition of Tantra, it's possible to clear out the chakra by repeating the mantra and focusing on the location of the chakra, in this case the throat.

Making Time for Meditation

In my workshops, the most common question is how to make time for meditation or how to create a ritual or daily practice. Most people want to be able to sit for thirty minutes, and that's a great goal, but if you're just starting out that's going to feel more like a burden than a jolt of calm. In the beginning, try meditating for just five minutes. Do this for a week and see how you feel. As you start to get more comfortable and feel and see the benefits, you'll want to sit for longer. Do what feels right for you. Some days I'll sit for ten minutes; other days it could be thirty.

Meditation is a practice that affirms all the steps of communicating like a Buddhist, which is why I've created guided meditations to go along with each chapter. You can download them for free by going to http://communicate likeabuddhistmeditations.com. Most of these are five- to ten-minute meditations.

Thought Process of Communicating Like a Buddhist

That which we persist in doing becomes easier for us to do; not that the nature of the thing is changed, but that our power to do is increased.

—Ralph Waldo Emerson

You've made it through the last step, and my hope is that if you've been doing the Cultivate Communication exercises within the chapters that you've made some strides toward changing how you communicate with others and yourself. As I said before, this is a lifelong process. But if you continually follow these five steps in all your interactions it will soon become a way of life.

As you use the steps, you'll notice your thought process is constantly going through the same cycle of questioning. I've highlighted that process here as a guide to help you on your way to more mindful communication. No matter the issue, the questions are the same, and they will help you keep the elements of right speech intact as you communicate with yourself and others.

1) Listen to Yourself
Is my self-talk and how I speak to others kind, honest, and free from judgment?Are my words enhancing the situation?

2) Listen to Others
Am I listening in a kind, honest, nonjudgmental, and helpful way? Am I putting myself in the other person's position? What experiences are influencing his or her perspective? What is the feeling behind his or her story? What does this person need to feel safe?

3) Speak Consciously, Concisely, and Clearly
Am I being clear and direct?

4) Silence as Speech
Is my silence kind, honest, judgment-free, and helpful?

You now know how to listen intently to others and to yourself, and how to choose your words skillfully so that the recipient is more likely to hear and understand you. You no longer speak negatively about people. You speak from the heart, and once the words are said, you let them go, knowing that someone else's response is not your responsibility. With all that you now know you have the tools to communicate like a Buddhist. My hope is that with these tools you move away from conversation rooted in reaction and toward conversation based on calmness, clarity, and cooperation.

I'd love to hear about how incorporating these steps has changed your communication routine and also if any shifts happen within your life because of them. Please reach out to let me know how it's going or if you have questions at cynthia@cynthiakane.com.

Acknowledgments

First and foremost I'd like to thank Susie Pitzen, because without her this book wouldn't have been possible. Susie, thank you for reaching out and for asking me the question I dreamed to hear: "Have you ever thought of writing a book?" Thank you Randy Davila for believing in this work and for giving me permission to go deeper, to let go so I could be myself within these pages. I am honored to have worked with such a thoughtful and inspiring team. Thank you.

Thank you to Nathaniel Branden for your work on self-esteem and to the late Marshall Rosenberg for your work on Nonviolent Communication. Your words have changed my life. Another life-shaping moment was the workshop I took with Terri Cole and Ashley Turner— thank you for giving me the tools needed to introduce me to myself.

To my brainstorming buddies, Susan Solomon and Ingrid Nilsen, not only would this book not be what it is without the two of you, but also my world wouldn't be the same without you in it. Thank you for helping me see clearly and live lightly.

Thank you to my mom and dad for teaching me that life is what we make it and for believing in me even when I wasn't able to. Your constant love and support energizes me to live each moment. I love you. To my sister and her amazing family, thank you for reminding me to laugh, play, jump, and blow bubbles—all the things that matter most.

Bryan, what can I say? You keep me present; you keep me grounded; you create such a warm, open, and loving environment that I feel truly comfortable expressing myself. Thank you for being such a beautiful addition to my life and for making me want to be the best version of me there is every day. I weird you big.

Resources

In writing this book, I studied the work of many of the best communication and Buddhism teachers. I've read every item listed below, and each has transformed the way I communicate and interact with the world. If I've been able to take pearls of wisdom and apply them from these sources, I'm confident you will too.

What's Your Communication Style?

The Art of Communicating by Thich Nhat Hanh

Insight Meditation: The Practice of Freedom by Joseph Goldstein

Radical Acceptance: Embracing Your Life with the Heart of a Buddha by Tara Brach, PhD

Fully Present: The Science, Art, and Practice of Mindfulness by Susan L. Smalley, PhD, and Diana Winston

Broken Open by Elizabeth Lesser

Loving-Kindness: The Revolutionary Art of Happiness by Sharon Salzberg

Listen to Yourself

Comfortable with Uncertainty: 108 Teachings on Cultivating Fearlessness and Compassion by Pema Chödrön

Shambhala: The Sacred Path of the Warrior by Chögyam Trungpa

Schachter-Singer Theory of Emotion: http://www.psychwiki.com/wiki/The_Schachter-Singer_Theory_of_Emotion

The Sweet Spot: How to Find Your Groove at Home and Work by Christine Carter, PhD

The Power of Habit: Why We Do What We Do in Life and Business by Charles Duhigg

Listen to Others

The 5 Love Languages: The Secret to Love That Lasts by Gary Chapman

The Female Brain by Louann Brizendine, MD

Speak Consciously, Concisely, and Clearly

The Success Principles by Jack Canfield

Nonviolent Communication: A Language of Life by Marshall B. Rosenberg, PhD

Rework by Jason Fried and David Heinemeier Hansson

Oh, Sure! Blame It on the Dog! A Pickles Collection by Brian Crane

Codependent No More: How to Stop Controlling Others and Start Caring for Yourself by Melody Beattie

A Woman's Self-Esteem: Struggles and Triumphs in the Search for Identity by Nathaniel Branden

The Verbally Abusive Relationship: How to Recognize It and How to Respond by Patricia Evans

Daily Wisdom: 365 Buddhist Inspirations edited by Josh Bartok

Use the Language of Silence

The Five Keys to Mindful Communication Using Deep Listening and Mindful Speech to Strengthen Relationships, Heal Conflicts, and Accomplish Your Goals by Susan Gillis Chapman

The Four Agreements by don Miguel Ruiz

The Everything Guide to Chakra Healing: Use Your Body's Subtle Energies to Promote Health, Healing, and Happiness by Heidi E. Spear

How God Changes Your Brain: Breakthrough Findings from a Leading Neuroscientist by Andrew Newberg, MD, and Mark Robert Waldman

The Art of Doing Nothing: Simple Ways to Make Time for Yourself by Veronique Vienne and Erica Lennard

Mating in Captivity: Unlocking Erotic Intelligence by Esther Perel

Amy Cuddy's Ted Talk and Power Pose articles: http://www.ted.com/talks/amy_cuddy_your_body_language_shapes_who_you_are

http://www.businessinsider.com/power-pose-2013-5

Meditation

Simple, Easy, Every Day Meditation Method by Sarah McLean

Studies proving the benefits of meditation: http://news.harvard.edu/gazette/story/2011/01/eight-weeks-to-a-better-brain/

http://www.psyn-journal.com/article/S0925-4927%2810%2900288-X/abstract

The Buddha Walks into a Bar . . .: A Guide to Life for a New Generation by Lodro Rinzler

Susan Piver's Open Heart Project: http://susanpiver.com/2012/04/11/right/

Tara Brach's guided meditations: http://tarabrach.com/mtti/2013-08-11-TrueRefuge-Tonglen-GuidedMeditation.pdf

The Everything Guide to Chakra Healing: Use Your Body's Subtle Energies to Promote Health, Healing, and Happiness by Heidi E. Spear

Perfect Health: The Complete Mind/Body Guide by Deepak Chopra, MD

About the Author

Dominique Fierro Photography + Design

Cynthia Kane received her BA from Bard College and her MFA from Sarah Lawrence College. She is a certified meditation and mindfulness instructor dedicated to helping men and women change their communication routines so they feel understood at home and at work, in control of their words and reactions. She lives in Washington, DC and offers workshops and personal coaching. Visit her at www.cynthiakane.com.

books that inspire your body, mind, and spirit

Hierophant Publishing
8301 Broadway, Suite 219
San Antonio, TX 78209
888-800-4240

www.hierophantpublishing.com